Better Business Writing

THE SUNDAY TIMES

Better Business Writing

Timothy R V Foster

KOGAN PAGE | *CREATING SUCCESS*

This book is dedicated to Christopher and Lauren

Parts of this book were previously published as *101 Ways to Better Business Writing*, also published by Kogan Page
First published as *Better Business Writing* in 2002

Kogan Page Limited
120 Pentonville Road
London N1 9JN

© Timothy R V Foster, 2002

British Library Cataloguing in Publication Data

A CIP record for this book is available from the British Library.

ISBN 0 7494 3801 0

Typeset by Jean Cussons Typesetting, Diss, Norfolk
Printed and bound in Great Britain by Clays Ltd, St Ives plc

contents

introduction

In spite of this age of the Internet, the World Wide Web and digital everything, never has the need for excellence in written communications been greater. Never have effective writing skills been more in demand, in business, education or government. The trend to downsizing, outsourcing, rationalisation and, these days especially, self-employment, means that people who never thought of themselves as writers must now take on that task as well as all the other responsibilities they face.

The expression of ideas, events, procedures, problems, expectations, requests, explanations, proposals and the like has to be so clear that your reader will not only understand, but be inspired to respond in the desired manner. Your task as a writer is to convey information so as to achieve the result you intend.

Yet people today have shorter attention spans and more distractions than ever before. Competition for their involvement has never been so intense; the cost of error never so high. A message has never had to compete for attention, understanding and acceptance so much as it must now.

Furthermore, people are so accustomed to getting their information from television, computer screens and even, still, the wireless, that written communications face a big challenge. How do you get your audience to *read*, rather than just look at, your words. Busy people hate to read. Hence this book. Give yourself the time and space it deserves, because you need to write effectively. Don't you?

Table 0.1 *The communications purpose/medium matrix (see page 14)*

Medium/Purpose	Inform	News	Understand	Persuade	Reassure	Teach	Explain	Transact
advertisement	x			x	x			x
article	x			x	x		x	
backgrounder	x		x				x	
book	x			x		x	x	
brochure	x			x			x	
catalogue	x			x			x	x
e-mail	x	x		x	x		x	x
letter	x	x		x	x		x	x
manual	x		x			x	x	
multimedia	x			x			x	
newsletter	x	x		x	x		x	
notice board	x	x		x	x		x	
press release	x	x			x			
proposal				x			x	
Q&A/FAQs	x		x			x	x	
sign	x				x	x	x	
slides	x			x		x	x	
speech	x					x		
task description			x			x	x	
video script	x			x	x	x	x	
Web site	x	x	x	x	x	x	x	x

the need for better communication

READ THIS, IF YOU CAN:
The world of business today, as never before, as is no doubt so often said, has a permanently and constantly varying and often frequently articulated requirement to communicate effectively, and in a timely fashion, in a manner designed to attract, to appeal to and to hold onto the readers' interests, with an increasingly wide variety of different audiences, such as customers suppliers employees shareholders partners regulatory bodies etc. In order for the reader to understand this point, it might be helpful for him (or her) to take the time to review determine, and, consider, some of the type's of communication's requirement's that a typical buisness might face in a typical-business day or week or month (or year), ie:

- To make a proposal for funding a new previously not done before venture.
- Describe a process so that those involved in the process will better understand the process and what they are required do about the process.
- Try to explain the process in order that the layman can

develop a satisfactory efficacious understanding of its paradimes and protocols.

■ Making an announcement to prospective governmental, municipal, educational and commerciallyorientated purchasers of the forthcoming availability of a recently developed product ...

STOP! COME BACK!

By now, I must have lost you! Your eyes have glazed over. You try to get more comfortable to help ease the pain. This is a book about better writing? That was *terrible* writing! Relax. It was put there to make a point. I bet you've read tons of writing like that. Isn't it a *crime*!

This book is about writing well so as to achieve your desired result. As such, it must practise what it preaches. How can I rephrase what I've just said to get you enthusiastically in the boat, to 'partner' with me in improving your business writing skills? By involving *you* and bringing the language to *life*. By eliminating *abstractions* and making examples *real* and *tangible*. Try this:

If you're in business, look at the various communications needs you could face in a day:

■ to ask for funding for your new idea;
■ to show people how to carry out a task;
■ to launch a new product to these markets:
   – governmental;
   – municipal;
   – educational;
   – commercial...

Notice how much easier that is to read? It talks to *you*, not 'the reader'. It sets you up for the story by putting you in context ('If you're in business...'). There are fewer words; fewer multisyllabic words next to each other (... announcement to prospective governmental municipal educational and commercially orientated purchasers of the forthcoming availability of a recently developed product...). And there's no redundancy (... describe a process so that those involved in the process...). The Plain Language Commission (Martin Cutts, 29 Stoneheads, Whaley Bridge, Stockport SK23 7BB, Tel: [01663] 733177, Fax: [01663] 735135, Web site: www.clearest.co.uk) has had much success in recent years getting organisations to clean up their written documents. It will even 'badge' documents as conforming to its Clear English Standard, after vetting. This book has been so badged.

Criteria established by the Plain Language Commission to meet its standard are as follows (reproduced by permission):

Purpose

■ Is the purpose stated early and clearly?

Content

■ Is the information accurate, complete and relevant?
■ Does the information anticipate readers' questions and answer them?
■ Is a contact point stated for readers who want to know more?

Structure

■ Is the information well organised and easy for the readers to find their way through?
■ Are there appropriate headings and sub-headings?
■ Are paragraphs kept reasonably short?
■ Is there appropriate use of illustrations, diagrams, summary panels and flow charts?
■ If the document is being read by non-specialists, are any essential specialist terms defined?

Style and grammar

■ Is the writing clear and crisp, with a good average sentence length (say 15–20 words throughout the document) and plenty of active voice verbs?

- Is the writing free from pomposity and officialese, using mainly everyday language (no aforesaids, notwithstandings, commencements and inter alias)?
- Is the English grammatical and well punctuated?
- Overall, is the style appropriate to the audience?

Layout and design

- Does it look good?
- Is the type easily readable?
- Is there enough space between lines of type?
- Is there a clear hierarchy of headings?
- Does the design help readers navigate through the document?

observe the Plain English Code

The Plain English Code has been established by the Plain Language Commission. If you follow it, your readers will thank you. Here it is (reprinted by permission – © 1994 Words at Work):

I will:

- match my writing to the needs and knowledge of the readers, remembering that many of them will be baffled by official jargon and procedures;
- consider carefully the purpose and message before starting to write, remembering that clear writing can only stem from clear thinking;
- structure the document clearly, perhaps with lists, headings and a pithy summary of key points;
- try to write sentences that average 15–20 words;
- try to keep the word order simple by putting the doer early in the sentence and following it with an active voice verb;
- take pride in everyday English, sound grammar and accurate punctuation;
- use 'I', 'we' and 'you' to make the writing more human;
- maintain the flow by starting some sentences with link words like 'but', 'however', 'so' and 'because';
- use commands when writing instructions;

▓   cut verbiage (at this particular moment in time);
▓   tell customers and colleagues clearly, concisely and courteously what has happened, how the situation stands, and what they can expect next;
▓   test high-use documents with typical users.

match your writing to the readers

Who are you talking to? (That seems to sound better than 'to whom are you talking?', which is grammatically more correct, but more pedantic. Listen to the sound of your words.)

Who are these people? Employees? Customers? Your bank manager? Your boss? A journalist? Someone with a complaint? Someone seeking information? Someone you want to romance or persuade? You must have a clear picture of who your audiences are before you can write an effective communication to them.

It's easiest to write when you know the actual person who will read your words. Then you can imagine how they will respond to what you are saying. I always find it helpful to identify a member of the audience when I'm writing; a real person, ideally someone I know. If I don't know the right kind of person I use my imagination. Then when I'm writing I think of how that person will react to my words. I form a mental picture of the person reading the document and I imagine the comments they'd make to themselves as they read. Whenever you have to write something, write down a list of your audiences for that task.

categorise your audiences

Here's a list of typical business audiences:

Internal

▉ management:
 – board directors;
 – management committees, your boss;
▉ employees:
 – current;
 – potential;
 – previous, retirees.

External

▉ financial:
 – funding sources;
 – shareholders;
 – investment analysts;
▉ customers:
 – current;
 – potential;
▉ competitors;
▉ media:
 – business and financial;
 – trade;
 – general;
▉ community;
▉ general public;
▉ government and regulatory bodies.

You need to talk to them in different ways according to who they are and what they do. You must recognise their working conditions and pressures so that your communication will get right through the haze of their other concerns. What do you want them to do, think or feel? Where are they coming from?

understand your audiences

Look at the conditions and pressures of the audiences we've just reviewed. How should you act when communicating to them?

Management

▓ They have very little time and are usually impatient. Get to the point fast.

▓ They are preoccupied with many things. You're probably not 'top of mind'. They may have higher priorities than you. Put your item into the context of their 'big picture'.

▓ They want to be efficient. Have a bullet point *Executive Summary* on the first page. Don't keep them in suspense.

▓ They are not as well informed about technicalities or detail as you. Avoid jargon and assumptions.

▓ Their role is to plan, lead, organise and control. Make recommendations and suggest courses of action rather than seek advice. Make it easy for them to respond.

Employees

▓ Are they gung ho and loyal? Be enthusiastic. Celebrate the team. Wave the flag.

▓ Are they disillusioned and unhappy, with concerns about their future, job security, etc? Be reassuring.

▓ If you have good news: rejoice and congratulate.

▓ If you have bad news: clarify, be forthcoming. Never lie.

Financial

▓ Seeking funds? Be clear and show the numbers.

■ Good investment performance? Be enthusiastic.

■ Poor investment performance? Be enthusiastic. Talk about possibilities for improvement, if any. Never lie.

Customers

■ Existing satisfied customers? Treat them with respect. Treat them as partners. You and they are part of the team. You want your relationship to go on and on.

■ Unsatisfied customers need to be assuaged? Treat them with respect, but make amends. How can you show them things will get better? No excuses!

■ Potential customers? Offer a taste of the promise. Talk benefits, not features (see page 16). Sell the sizzle, not the steak (as the Americans say – the Brits say sell the sizzle, not the sausage).

Competitors

■ Never slam your competitors. Concentrate on what differentiates you from them – your unique selling proposition (USP).

Media

■ They are confronted by a continuous flow of data from all over the world. They must ask: 'Of all this *stuff*, what is the top story I can run, given deadline and space limitations?' Bear in mind they need to complete the story by a deadline. What they are looking for:
  - stories that will interest their key audiences;
  - an unusual or provocative angle;
  - ability to met the deadline;
  - accuracy, verified facts.

Community

▓ Either they love you or they hate you. You are part of the neighbourhood. Be a good citizen and act accordingly. Provide accessible means of contact and invite feedback.

General public

▓ Assume they don't know much about your story, but don't be condescending. Be open and friendly. Provide accessible means of contact and invite feedback here, too.

Government and regulatory bodies

▓ Buck-passing and bewilderment are common at the junior levels. Typically expect a run-around. It's always some other department. Find the core area of importance and competence at the most senior level and concentrate on that. Then treat as you would management, above.

understand how audiences work

When you are writing a document, the people in your *primary audience* are those who should *take direct action* as a result. By 'take direct action' I mean react, order, approve, understand, learn, agree – those kinds of behaviour. *Secondary* audience members are people who ought to know, if only for information, such as competitors. The people the primaries listen to are called *opinion formers* if they are going to be proactive about your message, or *influencers* if they're going to be more reactive. Then there are the *allies* of these people. The more specific you can be in identifying them, the easier it will be to communicate. Take this book as a subject, for example; the audiences are:

Primary
Potential users of the book, defined as:

■ business executives and knowledge workers;
■ government employees in equivalent roles;
■ small business managers/proprietors;
■ independent consultants;
■ self-employed people/freelancers;
■ public relations people, advertising copywriters;
■ teachers/students – GCSE, A-Level, NVQ, GNVQ, university;
■ libraries;
■ book clubs.

Secondary

■ competitive publishers.

Opinion formers
For example, reviewers in the media that reach these people, such as:

■ print:
    – magazines;
    – newspapers;
        – daily;
        – weekly;
■ broadcast:
    – radio;
    – TV.

... in these subjects:

■ general business;
■ PR/advertising/marketing/writing;
■ book trade.

Influencers

- ▓ British Council;
- ▓ Confederation of British Industry;
- ▓ Department of Trade & Industry;
- ▓ Federation of Small Businesses;
- ▓ Institute of Directors;
- ▓ Institute of Practitioners in Advertising;
- ▓ Institute of Public Relations;
- ▓ Plain Language Commission;
- ▓ The Marketing Council;
- ▓ Training and Enterprise Councils.

Allies

- ▓ audiences of the above media;
- ▓ directors/members/customers of influencer organisations.

understand the purposes of your communication

There are many *reasons* to communicate:

- ▓ to inform;
- ▓ to deliver news, good/bad;
- ▓ to understand;
- ▓ to persuade;
- ▓ to reassure;
- ▓ to teach;
- ▓ to explain;
- ▓ to transact.

understand the means of communication

There are many *ways* of communicating. Here's another list:

- advertisement;
- article;
- backgrounder;
- book;
- brochure;
- catalogue;
- CV/resumé;
- e-mail;
- letter;
- manual;
- multimedia;

- newsletter;
- notice board;
- press release;
- proposal;
- Q&A/FAQs;
- sign;
- slides;
- speech;
- task description;
- video script;
- Web site.

Table 0.1 on page 2 puts the above lists together. The communication tasks are described in the following paragraphs. You'll find more detail on the specific means of communication in Chapter 4.

communicating to inform

To inform means to announce, reveal, divulge, acquaint, apprise, notify, disclose, report, convey, recount... When you inform, your objective is to change the audience's understanding of a situation, to make them aware of a condition. Here are some examples of information communications:

Changes

- address;
- name;

▓ pricing;
▓ dates of an event;
▓ extent of parts support via warranty.

Announcements

▓ new appointments;
▓ new product lines;
▓ new relationships.

Facilities detail or reference data

▓ operating hours and locations;
▓ descriptions of exhibits at a museum or gallery.

When you are informing, you can use just about every means of communication, ranging from advertisements (how to return contaminated food packages to a supermarket, for instance) to videos (*Understanding The Highway Code*), from magazine articles ('Christmas decoration ideas') to notices ('Rules of this Cemetery') or signs (in a museum describing a work of art, for example).

communicating to deliver news

When you deliver news, your objective is to bring the audience up to date as soon as possible. The distinction between merely informing and delivering news is, of course, that news is time-sensitive. Straight *information* may not be news, it may have been around a long time – such as gallery opening hours, the location of an emergency hospital or train timetables. But *news* has just happened, like the latest budget proposals from the Chancellor of the Exchequer or a breakthrough in the treatment of AIDS.

News is communicated through short-lived or rapidly updateable media, such as daily newspapers, newswires, newsletters, TV or radio bulletins, notice boards or electronic media such as Teletext and the Internet. Once we had town criers. After the news has appeared, the media carrying it may then become archival, part of 'the record' for later reference and use in history books, documentaries and so on.

communicating to understand

The act of writing a lucid description of a situation will, in itself, help to clarify the points that need to be made and can often bring a fresh understanding. The discipline of laying out the key aspects in a logical order will help to identify gaps. See page 19 for more detail.

communicating to persuade

The need to persuade includes examples such as selling your bank manager on your business plan, pitching for business, motivating employees into cooperating with your quality programme and advertising a product or service, among many others. Your objective is to get the reader to agree to, or take, some action.

benefits

The secret of persuasive writing is to communicate from your audience's point of view, stressing 'what's in it for them' – the benefits to them of taking the desired action.

People don't buy products, they buy benefits. They don't buy a stereo, they buy 'beautiful sound'. They don't buy a video recorder, they buy 'freedom to watch TV on their own terms'.

Here is the secret for recognising a benefit from a feature, and for getting to the *ultimate benefit*. The ultimate benefit is the most compelling one, based on that specific feature. The secret is based on the word 'so'. All you do is make a statement about the product or service, and then say 'so... ?'. There needs to be a slight questioning inflection in your voice. And you keep saying 'so... ?' until you get to the ultimate benefit.

For example: 'This video recorder (VCR) has its own tuner, so... ? you can record a programme on one channel while you are watching one on another channel, so... ? you can run your life on your own terms, not on the dictates of a programme schedule, so... ? you can get more out of your time, and do what you want when you want, so... ? you can be free, so... ' When you run out of responses to the word 'so... ?', you should be at the ultimate benefit.

In some cases, there may be other benefits that are 'right', but are not necessarily directly applicable to the reader. These are often emotive issues, such as 'reducing crime', 'improving the quality of education', 'easing global warming', 'saving the whales', 'helping the homeless' and so on.

communicating to reassure

When you are communicating to reassure, your objective is to allay fears. 'It's all right folks. We have matters well in hand. You have nothing to worry about.' Such communications would be needed if there was a big media scare brought about, for example, by some unwitting politician shooting off their mouth, as was the case, with the egg/salmonella-poisoning-risk mess of the late 1980s, which nearly killed the egg farming business in the United Kingdom.

The communicator needing to reassure is usually some unfortunate entity who wants to make things 'perfectly clear', as Richard Nixon used to say. The message to the audience is something like: 'Even though you think *this*, and other seemingly knowledgeable people have supported it, things are not as they seem. The facts are *these*.'

The effectiveness of this type of communication is in direct proportion to the credibility, public image or perception of the reassurer. US pharmaceutical giant Johnson & Johnson, a highly regarded company, suffered poisoning of its best-selling drug Tylenol by an extortionist in the 1980s. Several people were killed. J&J withdrew the product and made the packaging tamper-proof. J&J then communicated the steps it had taken to safeguard future users and saw its Tylenol market share return to its pre-tampering levels.

Contrast this with the derision met by British Rail when it blamed late-running trains on 'the wrong kind of snow', or by the multiple 'green shoots of recovery' statements made by assorted Chancellors of the Exchequer in recent recessionary times.

Credibility is clearly the key to successfully communicating to reassure. So if you have to write such a message, ask yourself 'how credible is the sender?'. If the answer is 'not very', you need to evolve strategies to overcome this barrier.

Communicating to reassure demands honest statements of fact, with no fudging or excuses. The media are notoriously unforgiving and jaded, so any hint of a cover-up will be instantly exposed and noised about, further destroying the credibility sought. The facts should speak for themselves and be as certain as the law of gravity. Ideally, believable and independent third parties should be used to provide supporting statements.

Source Perrier destroying millions of full bottles of Perrier mineral water when there was a contamination scare was, in itself, a form of communication to reassure. Such messages are not always only written. Actions speak louder than words, it has been said.

communicating to teach

When you are teaching through your writing, your objective is to convey your knowledge to the reader in the most effective way possible. You want the reader to say, ideally after one reading, 'Got it!'. Having read your text, the reader should then be able to turn around and explain the situation clearly and accurately to another person so that they, too, will say 'Got it!'.

So when a reader needs to learn from you, you need to be absolutely *clear* and *logical* in your writing.

By being clear, I mean using familiar, simple words and simple sentence constructions. The reader should not have to go over the material again and again to understand what you mean. If you have to introduce new words that are relevant to the subject, explain their meaning at the first use or refer the reader to a glossary that you include.

By being logical, I mean being sequential in your descriptions, presenting facts and concepts in a logical order.

To help your reader understand your point, use diagrams and visuals wherever possible:

Table 1.1 *Communicating to teach*

use simple words, sentences	write logically
explain new words or use a glossary	be sequential in descriptions
	present facts and concepts in logical order
use diagrams and visuals	give examples, tests and quizzes

Give examples. Have a test or a quiz so that the person may experience the thinking necessary to develop an understanding. The best way to learn something is to do it. Can you imagine learning to fly an aeroplane or play the piano without handling the controls or keys and getting visual, aural and kinetic feedback? Why should learning facts and procedures be any different? When you give a test you cause the reader to abandon the listening mode and change to the action, experiential mode.

communicating to explain

What's the distinction between teaching and explaining? My dictionary defines 'teach' as to show how to do something; to give instructions to; to train; to give lessons to; to provide with knowledge, insight. The word 'explain' means to make clear, plain or understandable; to give the meaning or interpretation of; to expound; to account for; to state reasons for.

Let me explain my interpretation of the distinction. Teaching means imparting knowledge that becomes a permanent resource, such as riding a bicycle or spelling. Explaining means imparting knowledge that is not necessarily permanently acquired, such as showing how to set up your video to record a programme that will air tomorrow night from 9 to 10 pm on Channel 4, or giving a recipe for bouillabaisse (a French fish soup).

Once a car driver knows how to drive they never need a written reference to handle the controls, but will sometimes need to look at a map to navigate, or study the manual to check what the tyre pressure should be. Other examples of communications to explain include:

▓   how to change the carburettor on a Ford Fiesta;
▓   how to load your camera with film;
▓   what to do in the event of fire;
▓   how to return unsatisfactory goods and claim a refund;

■ how to apply for a new passport;
■ how to troubleshoot the database software on your computer.

Note that most of these communications are for reference, using short-term memory. Once the task has been completed, the reader may shift the detail out of memory, using long-term memory to store the knowledge of where to look it up next time it is needed.

So communications to explain follow the same precepts as communications to teach – clear language, logical descriptions and plenty of diagrams. But they don't need tests and quizzes.

A good way to write this sort of material is to imagine you were writing a recipe. A good recipe lists the ingredients and amounts required, the utensils needed and gives an idea of the time required for the key steps. Then it breaks the steps down into a logical flow, grouping them by subject (eg, preparation, cooking, post-cooking). Language is in commands (do this, heat that, measure this). What kind of recipe do we have here?

The result of this recipe will be delicious crispy fried potatoes that put the average fish and chip shop's offering to shame. The potatoes should be cut into chips, the larger the potato, the more chips will be available. About .5 cm square and as long as they come is good. For best results, the potatoes should be microwaved first. For four large potatoes, allow 12 minutes. The potatoes must, of course, be washed before being put in the microwave. Set the microwave on high. Don't peel the potatoes, the skins are delicious! Meanwhile, some oil (about 2 cm deep) should be heated in a saucepan over a moderately high flame. Also a sieve and a scoop will be required. Two large potatoes per person or pro rata is a good allowance. When the oil is good and hot, about one potato's worth of chips should be immersed in it and cooked over a high heat until golden brown. A warm place to store the chips already cooked while the remainder are cooking will be required. The chips should be stirred constantly while they are cooking, otherwise they tend to stick together. Drain, sprinkle with salt and serve immediately.

Is that how to explain something?

communicating to transact

Transaction communications include contracts, agreements, receipts and confirmations. As such they are very often legal documents – that is paperwork that can form the basis for lawsuits or claims in the future. Hence good legal advice is essential. If you have a document that makes certain commitments and these commitments are not kept, it's the document that sets the rules, within the framework of appropriate law. Did you say you would deliver the goods on Tuesday, March 12, 2002? Did you fail to deliver them as promised? You are in breach of contract. You can be sued and have to pay damages and costs. Things to watch for:

- ■ Date every page, spelling the month out.
- ■ Indicate the currency of all financial figures (GB pounds? US dollars? Euros?). Numbers (like the total amount) should be written out in words, as well as figures.
- ■ Don't rely on abbreviations unless they are explained.
- ■ Show which law has jurisdiction.
- ■ Skip legal jargon (notwithstanding, heretofore, *sub judice*).
- ■ Clearly identify who the players are (eg, 'the Agency means Aspidistra Advertising of [address]. The Client means Plumbago Publishing of [address]').
- ■ Clearly identify who is expected to do what and how you know it has been done.
- ■ Use plenty of headings to help the reader navigate through the text.

2

the need for structure

Structure means the manner of building, constructing or organ-
ising; the arrangement or interrelation of all the parts of a
whole; the manner of organisation or construction.

You'll need to have a good idea of the structure of your ultimate document before you start writing. This book, for
example, has as its structure a series of non-threatening, bite-
size, informative sections distributed within six chapters. The
chapters are the broad subject matters, such as 'the need for
better communication' and 'the need for structure'. The
sections are detailed chunks of information, such as 'understand your audiences' and 'understand how audiences work'.
The sections are presented in a logical sequence. At the end of
the book is a comprehensive index.

understand the reason for structure

As Earthlings, we operate according to certain conventions and
expectations. We expect certain things to happen when certain

cues take place. When the traffic lights turn red, we expect traffic to stop. When the telephone rings, we expect it to be answered. When we produce our boarding pass at the gate, we expect to be invited onto the airliner.

When we read a document, we expect to be able to navigate through it with ease, finding information presented in a readable way, so that when we put it down after reading it we get the message. Yet, how many times have your own expectations of reading satisfaction been destroyed by fuzzy structure, poor layout, and just general confusion? I venture you have been frustrated often.

Well now you are the writer. Now it's your turn to deliver. So you'd better make sure you understand the need for proper structure in any document you are writing.

Your readers want to know what your document is about, why they should read it and what action is expected of them as a result. They do not want to be daunted by a threatening layout containing acres of closely set type, with few headings, no visuals and a scant table of contents, if any.

understand the parts of structure

Here is a list of the key structural components in documents:

- ▓ title;
- ▓ subtitle;
- ▓ author/originator/publisher;
- ▓ table of contents;
- ▓ introduction/rationale/purpose;
- ▓ chapters/sections/parts;
- ▓ headings and sub-heads;
- ▓ numbering systems;
- ▓ bullet points;
- ▓ visuals;

▧ appendices;
▧ index.

the importance of a good title

The title of a document is very important. It is there to tell the reader what the piece is about. Ideally, it should be brief and benefit-oriented, telling what the reader will get from it in one glance. It should not just be a subject name. If you can't get the benefit into the title, get it into the subtitle (see below). Here are some poor and better versions of what I mean:

Poor title ... not this:	*Better title* ... but this:
Audiovisual presentations	How to prepare and run audiovisual presentations
Financial results	XYZ Corporation 2002 financial results
XYZ Corporation video network	Recommendation for implementation of XYZ Corporation video network
Introducing the XYZ ZG-1	Introducing the XYZ ZG-1 Zero Gravity-belt
Advertising	XYZ Corporation 2003 advertising plans

Avoid the temptation to be cute and clever in your title, unless you are writing a work of fiction. Your objective in writing the title is to inform the busy and distracted reader of the subject matter quickly and effectively, not to play a guessing game. However, I will give you permission to be a little cute if you have a good explanatory subtitle...

the importance of a good subtitle

The subtitle should make the benefit of the document crystal clear. It should support, amplify and clarify the title. Here's the result of a random perusal of the catalogue of my publisher, Kogan Page, in a quest for title/subtitle examples:

Changing Corporate Values
A guide to social and environmental policy and practice in Britain's top companies

101 Great Mission Statements
How the world's leading companies run their businesses

Know Your Customers!
How customer marketing can increase your profits

There's even a cute one:
Agreed!
How to make your management communication persuasive

Although I have been using books in these examples, the concept of a clear subtitle is just as valid in other kinds of document, such as proposals, reports and even memos. Your role is to help your readers, not mystify them.

naming the author/originator/ publisher

On or near the front of the document, you need to say who it is from. A business letter will be on letterhead. But it is surprising how often you see a business document, such as a report or programme outline, that has no sense of who created it. You could argue that the document is internal, so everybody knows who it is from. Oh yeah? Why the mystery? Thousands of so-called 'internal' documents get into the hands of external people, quite legitimately. For example, you are producing a brochure or briefing your ad agency, so you hand over a bunch of files for 'background reading'. In large organisations, the issuing department or division needs to be identified, as well. And, of course, the date of issue should be on the front page.

table of contents

The purpose of the table of contents is to help the reader navigate through the document and provide logical reference. Any document in excess of, say, six pages, should have some kind of table of contents. Write the contents with the readers in mind. Assume they are not as familiar with the subject as you are.

Producing the table of contents will help you to refine the document's organisation since it lays it out as a quick overview. Does it make sense the way you've assembled it? If not, fix it. It is a good idea to keep a running table of contents as you put the work together. Better to find out you need to reorganise the piece sooner rather than later.

The table of contents should reflect the structure of the document. Here's an excerpt from the contents of this book:

Contents

Another approach is to give a brief summary of each section, and its source, if relevant. Here's an excerpt from my book *Winning Ways for Business in Europe*:

the introduction

The introduction sets the stage, provides the rationale and purpose for the document. It provides a context for the reader. Maybe it summarises the contents. Reread the introduction to this book (page 1) as an example.

chapters/sections/parts

A chapter is any of the main divisions of a book or other writing. Outside of books, you may find the term *section* is used. Chapters group subject matter into relevant, cohesive segments. Here's how the chapters are organised in my book *101 Ways to Get Great Publicity*:

1 Understanding the basics about publicity
2 Improving your image
3 Understanding the basics of media relations
4 Creating your own media
5 Involving others in your message
6 Designing special events
7 Using stunts to get ink
8 Dealing with adverse publicity

Parts are usually senior to chapters. Parts take massive sections of text and divide them into manageable portions. For example, Kogan Page's book *Marketing Communications* (by P R Smith and Jonathan Taylor) is organised into two parts: *Part 1, The background to the communications process*, divided into nine chapters, and *Part 2, The marketing communication tools*, broken down into a further eleven chapters.

headings and sub-heads

Headings and sub-heads break down long segments of text into smaller sections. The sections so derived are too small to be chapters or major sections on their own. They reside within the broader section as little, coherent units of text. Headings are 'senior' to sub-heads and usually cover larger segments than sub-heads. There may be sub-sub-heads. You'll need to pick a style of typography for each item so the reader can easily tell the difference.

Kogan Page, publisher of this book, gives instructions for the preparation of the manuscript (ms) and says this about headings:

In order to distinguish between levels of heading use the following variations in type:

- ▓ chapter titles:
  full caps, underlined (LIKE THIS);
- ▓ A-level headings:
  full caps (LIKE THIS);
- ▓ B-level headings:
  upper-case initial only, underlined (Like this);
- ▓ C-level headings:
  upper-case initial only (Like this);
- ▓ D-level headings:
  upper-case initial, italic *(Like this).*

See the Vobis example on page 31.

making sub-heads work

One way to determine if your headings and sub-heads work is to read them sequentially without paying attention to the body copy in between. Do they tell the story on their own? If they do, they work well. If they don't, maybe they should be changed.

writing style in heads is important

Grammatically, headings are seldom sentences. A heading can be one word, eg, *Budget*. However, it's a good idea to make the grammatic sense of a *sequence* of headings work together. Thus when the headings are read one after the other on their own they tell a story. For example, a report on cost reduction plans might have headings like:

Situation
Current cost base
Staffing levels

... etc. To suddenly throw in a heading that reads:

How we intend to reduce costs

... is interruptive of the overall style. Better the line should reflect the style of the other headings, such as:

Cost reduction plans

Alternatively, the overall style could go the other way:

Where we are today
Where the money is going
Our people situation

... here, *Cost reduction plans* would interfere with the style.

In a large document watch out for the common mistake of having several headings similarly named. You can avoid this by staying away from generalities, like *Miscellaneous*, and aiming at more specific headings, such as *2002 Staffing Levels*. Below is an example of the use of headings and sub-heads from my book *Winning Ways for Business in Europe*. It starts with a major heading which, in this case, is underlined. The sub-heads are not underlined.

(There's no rule about typographical styles for different headings. It's whatever you decide. As mentioned above, many companies have style books that dictate this kind of detail.)

Vobis: Putting Flexibility and Speed to Work
by Theo Lieven

Vobis is the largest personal computer (PC) retailer in Europe. We have over 200 branches in Germany, The Netherlands, Belgium, Italy, Austria, Spain, Luxembourg, Poland, France and Switzerland. We also manufacture our own systems under the Highscreen brand. In 1992, we outsold IBM PCs in Germany two to one – a total of 320,000 Highscreen PCs were sold in that year making us number one. We have 16 per cent of the market in Germany. Our turnover in 1992 was DM 1.5 billion, up 53 per cent on 1991 and our 1992 profits were DM 60 million before tax.

Flexibility and speed

Flexibility and speed are the words that define our organisation. Flexibility and speed belong together. With low speed you cannot be flexible. In fact, I hear that there are two kinds of company: the speedy, fast ones and the dead!

What do I mean by speed? It's how fast you can react to the needs of the marketplace and deliver what is wanted. Speed is of the essence.

The future is very close in our business, maybe six months out. We don't need five years to design a new product, as they seem to in the car business. A computer takes six or nine months for most manufacturers, and far less for us. As soon as the parts are available we buy them in small quantities, put them together and see how the new design works in the marketplace.

Introducing a new computer

It goes like this. A new development evolves in computer hardware, perhaps a new CPU (central processing unit) chip, an improved LCD (liquid crystal display) screen or a better high-density hard disk drive. Let's say it will be ready for shipment from the Far East in nine months time. Computer manufacturers see an opportunity for a new product based on this improvement, say a refined notebook computer. So they put their ideas together and start the process of new-product development.

numbering systems

We now come to the subject of text numbering. You'll most often find numbering in legal documents and manuals. The reason for numbering text chunks is to facilitate reference to specific sections later in the document, or in citations in other documents. Numbering formats include these:

1, 2, 3	Arabic numbers
I, II, III	upper-case roman numerals
A, B, C	upper-case letters
i, ii, iii	lower-case roman numerals
a, b, c	lower-case letters

My '101 Ways' books, published by Kogan Page, use a very simple numbering format. They have chapters and 'ways'. Since the ways run consecutively through the book, it is only necessary to cite a way number for reference, eg, see Way 24. There is no need to say see Chapter 2, Way 24. The chapters are there to organise groups of ways into broader subject areas.

My preference is to avoid using roman numerals. I, II and III are fine. But what on earth is CLIX? (Actually, it's 159.)

understanding civil service text numbering

1. The whole-hog approach to text numbering is known as the Civil Service System.

2. In this, each paragraph is numbered from start to finish.

3. Usually each chapter or section is also numbered. So a reference to a paragraph in such a book might be 2.26.4 (Chapter 2, 26th section, paragraph 4).

The major drawback in using numbering systems is in the assembly and editing process. If you number every section, every chapter, every paragraph and every bullet point, you could end up with a reference like this: 2.1.3.1.5. This might mean, for example, part 2, chapter 1, paragraph 3, bullet point 1, sub-point 5. Aaargh! Now what happens if, before you go to press, you insert a new paragraph before this, and two new earlier sub-points in the relevant bullet point? It all changes to 2.1.4.1.7. And all the succeeding paragraph numbers must change. And all the references throughout the document must be checked and corrected, if necessary – every time you make a change. So number every paragraph at your peril. Sophisticated word-processing software can handle the task of maintaining numbering logic, or at least make the task of changing everything easier, however. But you have to know how to use it, or it'll get worse.

know when to use bullet points

In this era of minuscule attention spans and quick cutting, as typified by MTV rock videos, many people are frightened of vast areas of text. A popular solution is to put the message into bullet points. Bullet points:

■ are less daunting than large blocks of text;
■ are easier to read;
■ convey the point quickly;
■ work well in expressing complicated ideas;

■ are ideal when communication is relatively informal;
■ need to be broken up with text every so often;
■ should not be used where narrative text works better.

Bullet points should be used for emphasis, or when you need to explain something complex. And they should be used for lists.

You would not normally see an entire text in bullet points, except in a presentation document, as used to support a new-business pitch or proposal. Hence you'll also find bullet points used extensively in copy on slides, transparencies or a computer presentation (see page 115).

sequence bullet points intelligently

The sequence in which bullet points appear is important. The information should flow logically. If there is no particular logic, eg, when you're running a *list*, try alphabetical order. Or maybe it makes sense to present the list in chronological order, or arranged geographically.

example of logical flow

This is taken from my book *101 Ways to Generate Great Ideas*. It is a list of reasons why a project could fail and is presented in basic order of likelihood of occurrence:

What are the barriers to success? Here are some examples:

■ production delays;
■ errors in development;
■ catastrophe (fire, earthquake, war);
■ weather problems (too hot/too cold/too wet/too dry/too windy);
■ strikes/industrial action;
■ cost overruns;

- competitive pre-emption;
- changes in laws (regulation/taxes);
- financial problems;
- staff training problems;
- business failure of distributor or retailer;
- economic conditions (high unemployment/interest rates/ stock-market crash);
- poor advertising results;
- public apathy.

example of chronological flow

Objective – get driver's licence:

- read *The Highway Code*;
- obtain provisional driver's licence;
- ask for literature from driving schools;
- go and talk to schools;
- establish budget and timetable;
- enrol in driving school;
- take driving lessons;
- build experience, practise skills;
- study *The Highway Code*;
- pass written exam;
- pass driving test;
- obtain driver's licence.

See how useless the above would be if presented alphabetically?
Objective – get driver's licence:

- ask for literature from driving schools;
- build experience, practise skills;
- enrol in driving school;
- establish budget and timetable;
- go and talk to schools;
- obtain driver's licence;
- obtain provisional driver's licence;

- ■ pass driving test;
- ■ pass written exam;
- ■ read *The Highway Code*;
- ■ study *The Highway Code*;
- ■ take driving lessons.

example of alphabetical flow

On the other hand, straight, non-hierarchical lists benefit from alphabetical sequencing. There are many *ways* of communicating:

- ■ advertisement;
- ■ article;
- ■ backgrounder;
- ■ book;
- ■ brochure, etc, etc.

example of geographical sequence

It may be helpful to show your list arranged geographically. This example is arranged west to east, as you would look at it on a map. Canada's provinces:

- ■ British Columbia;
- ■ Alberta;
- ■ Saskatchewan;
- ■ Manitoba;
- ■ Ontario;
- ■ Quebec;
- ■ New Brunswick;
- ■ Prince Edward Island;
- ■ Nova Scotia;
- ■ Newfoundland.

This might work better than an alphabetical listing, since alphabetically the provinces are not shown contiguously, making things like distribution patterns, time zones, etc harder to grasp. Canada's provinces:

■ Alberta;
■ British Columbia;
■ Manitoba;
■ New Brunswick;
■ Newfoundland;
■ Nova Scotia;
■ Ontario;
■ Prince Edward Island;
■ Quebec;
■ Saskatchewan.

If you are making a list of, say, branch offices, you could present it alphabetically by city:

■ Amsterdam;
■ Athens;
■ Brussels;
■ Budapest;
■ Copenhagen;
■ Frankfurt;
■ Helsinki;
■ London, etc, etc.

But note that the sequence changes if you go alphabetically by country:

■ Austria, Vienna;
■ Belgium, Brussels;
■ Czech Republic, Prague;
■ Denmark, Copenhagen;
■ Finland, Helsinki;
■ France, Paris;

■ Germany, Frankfurt;
■ Greece, Athens, etc, etc.

If you often confront this issue, pick a style (*either* city *or* country, not 'whatever') and stick to it; it will make life easier for you.

sorting by the most important factor

A European telephone dialling code listing could be presented two ways. Alphabetically by location:

■ Albania   355;
■ Andorra   33 628;
■ Austria   43;
■ Belgium   32;
■ Denmark   45.

Or numerically by dialling code:

■ 30   Greece;
■ 31   Netherlands;
■ 32   Belgium;
■ 33   France;
■ 34   Spain.

Which way would be most useful? Obviously, it depends on the need. The point is, you should always figure out the reader's need and design your output accordingly.

know when not to use bullet points

Here's an example of how narrative text can tell the story

better than bullet points, from my book *101 Ways to Get More Business*:

> My hardware store recently started opening for a short time on Sundays, because the new video-rental store next to him did so. I asked the owner if it was worthwhile. 'Definitely. And I've got a very selfish reason for saying that. The revenues we produce in the two hours we're open on Sunday give me enough to enable me to hire a part-timer to come in on Mondays – a fairly slow day – and enable me to take a day off! But most important, we're open when our customers want us to be open.'

You can see that a bullet point version of this text would be somewhat laboured, in fact, wrong!

use bullet points correctly

Bullet points must be crafted carefully:

- taking text that you would normally write as straight prose, and;
- sticking a bullet point in front of each sentence, as we are doing here;
- is not the answer;
- bullet points have their own style of language and structure.

Let's rewrite the above and see how bullet points work:

- bullet points have own style:
  - language;
  - structure;
- normal prose style unsuitable.

If you're writing a series of bullet points, avoid these mistakes:

- starting the first bullet point like this, then;

- avoid the mistake of changing the tense of the verb;
- sometimes no verbs;
- never do it like that!

Rewriting the above into a better style, we would see:

- Establish a style for bullet points.
- Stick to style all the way.
- Example: start each bullet point with active verb.
- How messy it becomes if you don't do this!

use bullet points to reduce word/page count

Sometimes you need to keep the overall number of words down in a document, to reduce reading time or space needed. Bullet points help you do this. Let's see how:

- Bullet points help keep word count down.
- Bullet points enable you to write more tightly.
- Bullet points help keep page count down.
- Bullet points telegraph their ideas to the reader.

Get it? We don't, in fact, need to keep repeating the words 'bullet points'. The above ideas are expressed better like this. Bullet points:

- help keep word count down;
- enable you to write more tightly;
- help keep page count down;
- telegraph their ideas to the reader.

However, to make sure you've written them correctly, always go back and read them again, testing the sense by reading each point to yourself, along with its unspoken header, one by one, like this. Bullet points:

■ help keep word count down;
Bullet points:
■ enable you to write more tightly;
Bullet points:
■ help keep page count down;
Bullet points:
■ telegraph their ideas to the reader.

In this way you would catch a mistake like:
Bullet points:

■ enables you to write tighter;
■ helps keep page count down.

pick a bullet point style and stick to it

Bullet points should be laid out in a standard format throughout the piece. Note how we are doing them in this book. My preference is for bullet point text to be indented if it runs longer than one line, like this:

■ My preference is for bullet point text to be indented if it runs longer than one line, like this is.
■ Bullet point text running longer than one line and not indented is harder to read.
■ Your word-processing software can handle the indenting task with ease.

Many people, including me, prefer to start each bullet point with a capital letter; others prefer to use lower-case letters. My preference is not to punctuate each bullet point, although sometimes it is necessary to do so. Some people put full stops or semi-colons at the end of each bullet point line. Kogan Page, the publisher of this book, uses capital letters and full stops where there are complete sentences in bulleted lists, otherwise, lower case and semi-colons. Whatever you do, be consistent, certainly within chapters or sections.

Sub-points of bullet points should be further indented, as in this book. I prefer to use a dash instead of a bullet for sub-points. Some use other devices, such as a + sign, for example:

■ This is the first line:
  – This is the first sub-point.
  + This is the first sub-sub-point.

number the bullet points only if it helps

My preference is to avoid numbering bullet points. It tends to create a hierarchy that may be artificial. But if you are listing sequential action steps, numbering makes sense, eg:

How to change a tyre:

1. Pull car off road and set parking brake.
2. Turn on flashers and set up warning triangle.
3. Remove spare tyre, jack and tools from boot... etc, etc.

If you need to constantly refer to specific points, as in a 'how-to' manual, numbering can be helpful. If you find you have sub-points, it makes the numbering much more complex. This is called the decimal system:

1. This is the first line of a major point.
   1.1 This is the first sub-point of bullet 1.
       1.1.1 This is the first sub-point of 1.1.
   1.2 This is the second sub-point of bullet 1.
2. This is the first line of bullet 2.
   2.1 This is the first sub-point of bullet 2.
       2.1.1 This is the first sub-point of 2.1.

use visuals

One picture is worth a thousand words, they say. So use visuals whenever possible. Visuals include photographs (in colour or monotone), graphic renderings, cartoons, diagrams, charts (see Chapter 4), maps, layouts and even typographical devices called dingbats. I have a font called Zapf Dingbats on my Macintosh, which gives all kinds of useful symbols. Here are some of them:

using dingbats

You can select dingbats and combine them with regular text to create special graphic elements to dress up your work. For example, if you really want your bullet points to stand out, how about these?

✈ three non-stop flights a day from Heathrow;
✈ comfortable Boeing 757 service with seat-back video entertainment system;
✈ business class available for only £50 more per ticket.

using cartoons

Appropriate cartoons get attention and help to tell a story. You can use them to make a point or to provide a little light relief. If you have trouble finding a cartoonist, *The Creative Handbook*, published each year by Reed Information Services Ltd, has extensive listings of cartoonists, as well as illustrators, photographers and designers.

Figure 2.1 *Cartoons help get attention (cartoon by Ralph Schlegel)*

the role of appendices

Appendices are where you put background information and detail when you don't want it to get in the way of the flow of your overall document. They usually sit in the back of the document. If there is more than one, refer to them as Appendix 1, 2, etc. Here are the sorts of data that belong in an appendix:

- research statistics;
- historic data, eg, financial results, performance statistics;
- maps;
- tabular information, such as comparative analyses;
- bibliographies and reading lists;
- text that supports the main text, included for reference;
- useful addresses and other directories;
- branch office locations;
- names of subsidiary companies, dealers or representatives;
- regulatory information, eg, visa requirements;
- biographies of company executives involved in a project;
- lists of customers or projects undertaken.

when you need an index

Any business book or major document should be indexed. I am amazed at how often you see no index in a non-fiction book or, at best, a very perfunctory one. Good indices are part of the essential knowledge-navigation process. With computers, they are easy to do. There is no excuse for not having an index.

how to create an index on your computer

Wait until the ms is paginated correctly (if it is a book, that means when you have final page proofs). Using spreadsheet software, such as Microsoft Excel®, go through the ms and simply enter key words line by line in the first vertical column of the spreadsheet. In the next column to the right, enter the page number. Insert a new row in the correct alphabetical location each time you add a new key word. (The software enables you to sort the entries alphabetically in a few seconds, so it is easy to keep the worksheet in proper order as you progress.) I can usually do a full index in a few hours.

Table 2.1   *Example of an index spreadsheet*

	A	B
1	a-roll	58
2	activities day	87, 94
3	adverse publicity	99–108
4	advertisement	9
5	advertising	9, 10, 12, 35, 64

Sub-entries
You may have a major subject that deserves its own index entry, but that also warrants sub-entries. In this case, present the sub-entries in alphabetical order within the major entry:

Aircraft
   Aeronca Champion   22, 37
   Beagle Pup   45
   Beech Baron   3, 5, 9, 15
   Beech Bonanza   3, 6, 9, 15, 22, 27
   Cessna Citation   14, 57

the need for style

The most frequent criticism about business writing is that it is so often wordy, trite and hard to understand – in fact, just not readable. To wit, boring! Readable writing should be transparent. It should not interfere or call attention to itself. And it should be interesting. This chapter discusses writing style in more detail.

use personal text style where possible

Are you going to *talk* to the reader? Then you will talk about *you* a lot, as we are here. This makes what you have to say more interesting. Contrast this with: will your story address the reader in the third person? In such cases the reader may regard him or herself (awkward stuff) as the intended beneficiary of the words, but may not feel involved. Readers who are forced to sit through such third party formality may be excused if the double-glazing comes up before their eyes and they drift off into their own world. But don't mix styles between personal (you) and impersonal (the reader) a lot in the same piece. It gets confusing.

use active text styles where possible

Which text style would you prefer to read? 1) The possession of valid liability insurance is a legal requirement of all vehicle operators. 2) The law requires all vehicle operators to possess valid liability insurance.

The first one seems pompous and officious. The second seems natural and simple. The first is passive, the second is active. The active style is preferred by most people. In fact, most people prefer the active style.

When you want to write actively, put the doer up front. Follow this with the verb and end with the action. 'Harry (the doer) passed (the verb) his driving test (the action).'

The passive version turns this around, starting with the action, followed by the verb and ending with the doer: 'The driving test (the action) was passed (the verb) by Harry (the doer)'.

More examples:

Passive
The new TV commercials will be produced by the ad agency.
Active
The ad agency will produce the new TV commercials.

Passive
A 10p-off price incentive will again be offered to purchasers.
Active
Purchasers will again be offered a 10p-off price incentive.

Passive
Longer sentences and more words are used in the passive construction (11 words).
Active

The passive construction uses longer sentences and more words (nine words).

know when to use the passive style

Sometimes there are moments when the passive style can work better. It might be preferable to use it when you want to emphasise a point: 'No fatalities were experienced last year by Britain's airlines'. 'The Police have been praised once again with the announcement of a reduction in drink-driving arrests for the second year in a row.'

The insertion of the occasional sentence in the passive style can also liven up the writing and combat boardroom boredom. But my advice is keep the ratio of active to passive high.

avoid verbosity – keep it simple, stupid (KISS)

There is a particular and continually self-evident tendency among some writers, especially those writing for business or academic audiences, such as professors and management executives and those who sit on boards of directors and other important committees, to construct sentences of enormous complexity, such as that which has been composed in this particular location as an advantageous example, to bring the concept home forcefully, as it were, and use a vastly increased, relative to what is necessary, quantity of extraordinarily lengthy and time-consuming-to-read, let alone absorb, words, such as adjectives, adverbs, nouns, verbs (always, of course, it goes without saying, conjugated in their correct and relevant tenses), pronouns (personal and occasionally, as required by the text, impersonal), conjunctions and other parts of speech as may be experienced when attempting to comprehend good grammatical practices by reference to one of the more acceptable literary textbooks (titles of which the writer is, regretfully, not at liberty to divulge for fear that he be accused of favouritism), and often with extensive quantities of irrelevant sub-clauses and sub-sub-clauses, which only have a tendency to obfuscate the sense and veritable meaning the communicator is attempting to have conveyed in written, as opposed to verbal, or oral, as it is so often termed, terms.

For heaven's sake get to the point early. Avoid long sentences and long paragraphs. Avoid lots of polysyllabic words running together.

avoid redundancies and also unnecessary words, too

Part of the complexity of the problem with verbosity, wordiness and excess verbiage comes from the not uncommon tendency for individual people to use too many extra unnecessary words that are definitely not needed to make the actual clarity of the specific communication crystal clear.

Let's rewrite that sentence, cutting out the verbiage: 'Verbosity is the use of more words than necessary for clear communication'. We've gone from 45 words to 12. In the above example, the verbosities come from:

- ■ redundant words, eg:
    - part of the complexity of the problem;
    - verbosity, wordiness and excess verbiage;
    - definitely;
- ■ extraneous adjectives, eg:
    - *excess* verbiage;

- *individual* people;
- *extra* unnecessary words;
- *actual* clarity;
- *specific* communication;
- *crystal* clear;

■ double negatives, eg:
- not uncommon.

When you have written something, read it with a view to eliminating verbosity. Then cut out the deadwood.

use words well

When you pick words, simplicity and clarity are critical. Use words that are easy to understand, concrete and precise, which express the exact meaning you want to convey. This should not restrict you to the one-syllable words of the preschooler, but you must avoid stilted words and lofty, abstract writing. When choosing words, select the:

■ familiar vs the unfamiliar;
■ short vs the long;
■ single word vs the circumlocution;
■ concrete vs the abstract;
■ precise vs the vague.

Familiar vs unfamiliar
Use:

■ active vs peripatetic;
■ early vs inchoate;
■ hung over vs crapulous;
■ modern vs neoteric;
■ tireless vs indefatigable.

Short vs long
Use:

- briefly vs momentarily;
- chance vs happenstance;
- easy vs uncomplicated;
- right vs appropriate;
- simple vs straightforward.

Single word vs circumlocution
Use:

- delay vs hold in abeyance;
- never vs not under any circumstances;
- now vs at this particular moment in time;
- quickly vs without wasting any further days;
- yes vs in the affirmative.

Concrete vs abstract
Use:

- about vs relating to the situation regarding;
- door vs entranceway;
- radio, TV vs broadcast media;
- tell vs advise in regard to;
- train, bus vs public transportation facilities.

Precise vs vague
Use:

- turbofan vs motor;
- Alsatian vs police dog;
- 1600 hours vs the afternoon;
- 25p stamp vs postage;
- Internet vs information superhighway.

use simple sentence architecture

When constructing sentences, follow these general principles:

- Keep most sentences short, simple and direct:
  - vary sentence length and structure somewhat for interest and change of pace;
  - the ideal average sentence length is 15–20 words.
- Convey only one or two main thoughts in each sentence:
  - use proper emphasis to show the relative importance of ideas within a sentence.
- Don't complicate the sentence by including a number of qualifications or conditions:
  - use separate sentences (and use parenthetical expressions sparingly).
- Make certain that relationships (subject to verb) are clear in each sentence.
- Use enough conjunctions and transitional phrases to ensure smooth reading.

use paragraphs properly

The paragraph, while it breaks the text into more readable units, also helps your reader by grouping sentences around a central idea and developing that idea.

Include a topic sentence to summarise the entire paragraph or introduce its subject. Then support this with a statement giving reasons or facts that make the point. Use specific examples or details to explain or clarify. Eliminate any extraneous or irrelevant material. Follow a logical sequence in explaining or supporting the topic sentence.

Avoid long paragraphs. Three to five sentences per paragraph are about right. One-sentence paragraphs are allowed, too.

use apostrophe's, oops, apostrophes, properly

I am constantly amazed at how often you see mistaken uses of apostrophes. The problem all boils down to different relationships with the letter s at the end of a word. These can happen three ways:

■ to pluralise a word – Tom, Dick and Harry or three Harrys;
■ to create contractions of verbs like 'is' – Harry's going to get fired if he keeps doing that;
■ to denote possessiveness – Harry's new car is a Mercedes.

So why do you keep seeing signs with these pluralisations?

■ 'Scallop's for sale'.
■ 'Ticketholder's this way'.
■ 'Egg's 60p per dozen'.

The only time you would use an apostrophe with an s for a plural would be when it is needed for clarification, thus: There are four i's in the word 'initiation'.

You don't put an apostrophe before the s in other pluralisations. Some people seem to think if singular nouns end in a vowel they get apostrophes when they go plural. Or a brand name should get one when pluralised. Not so. It's:

■ cameras   not camera's;
■ torsos   not torso's;
■ Hondas   not Honda's;
■ Elegantes   not Elegante's;
■ Hitachis   not Hitachi's;
■ Scorpios   not Scorpio's;
■ Subarus   not Subaru's.

Another popular misconception is to apostrophise abbreviations, acronyms, dates or foreign words when pluralising. Not so. It's:

- Ps and Qs   not P's and Q's;
- plcs   not plc's;
- Q&As   not Q&A's;
- the '60s   not the '60's;
- matinées   not matinée's.

its and it's

There's this creepy little word that has its own rules. It's 'it':

- When it's possessive, it's its, *without* an apostrophe.
- When it's plural it's its, *without* an apostrophe.
- When it means it is or it has, it's it's, with an apostrophe.

possessives for words ending in 's'

If the word ends in s already, you make it possessive by putting the apostrophe after the s. You can then add another s if it sounds right to you:

- the Mercedes's automatic transmission;
- Charles's wedding;
- the three princesses' tiaras;
- Chambers' new dictionary;
- the Joneses' new TV set.

Exceptions are pronouns such as ours, yours, his, hers or theirs. All these are possessive, but they take no apostrophe.

contractions

Apostrophes are also used to denote contractions, such as can't (cannot), won't (will not), doesn't (does not), he'll (he will), I'll (I will), you're (you are), one o'clock (one of the clock), etc. A very common error is to mean 'you are', intend 'you're' and write 'your', as in 'Your going to the dinner in your car or mine?'

use hyphens properly

Hyphens cause problems mostly when they are not used. I'm talking about compound adjectives, ie, two adjectives next to each other describing the same noun. For example, if you ran an advertisement looking for a second-hand boat as: 'Wanted: little used boat' there could be some confusion. Are you looking for a second-hand boat that's not very big, or one that has not been used very much? The former meaning takes no hyphen. The latter should have a hyphen thus: 'Wanted: little-used boat'. Little-used is a compound adjective.

A popular phrase in today's business writing is 'state of the art'. When should it be hyphenated and when not? Try these:

- ▓ Our offices have state-of-the-art communications systems.
- ▓ Our telephone and computer interface is state of the art.

As well as in compound adjectives, you'll find the hyphen used in other compound constructions, such as anti-smoking, pro-bono, non-acceptable, pre-empting, ex-husband, and semi-comatose.

make sure the tense agrees with the subject

You see this mistake a lot, too. I'm talking about agreement between plurals and singulars, verbs and nouns. Sentences like this has often been found, even on the BBC news. And sometimes a sentence like this have.

Here are two examples from just one article in today's *International Herald Tribune*: 'The quality of living standards are different from one place to another'. Six paragraphs later, we are greeted with: 'The toy department of stores in Beijing's fashionable Wangfuling Street have been jammed with shoppers…'.

The problem often occurs when a plural noun precedes a verb that refers to an earlier, singular noun, particularly in speech. You often hear a quote like this on the evening news: 'The Chancellor said the prevailing interest rate, in spite of the record over the last three years, were lower than it should be, so he raised it by one point'. The flip side, happens, too, of course: 'The Chancellor said prevailing interest rates, in spite of the record over the last year, was lower than they should be, so he raised it by one point'. Doesn't it scream out? So why do it keep happening? Oops.

understand UK/US differences

Which brings us to the great cultural divide known as the Atlantic Ocean. In the United States, companies, brand names and entities are usually singular. A company is singular. So is Congress. So is British Airways, which used to have as its slogan 'British Airways takes good care of you'. 'Coke is it.' But in the United Kingdom, companies and entities are often plural. Brand names seem to go either way. ('Coke are them?' – No!) 'Lillets provide protection' (in the United States, 'Lillets provides protection'). 'Fairy washes cleaner'. England are not going to win the World Cup this year. 'British Airways take good care of you'. Parliament are having a rough time this session. In the United States a company is usually 'it'. In the UK, a company is (are?) usually 'they'. Pick one style and stick to it in your text.

Alfred Hitchcock had fun with this business when he launched his 1963 movie *The Birds*. The teaser line, in perfect English? '*The Birds* is coming!' And *Encyclopedia Britannica* uses the tagline '*Dick & Jane* is dead', which is correct because here Dick & Jane is a single entity, namely a book title. See how the use of italics helps (helps because it's the *use* [singular] of italics doing the helping – otherwise it would be 'See how italics help', because *italics* [plural] are doing the helping). The common mistake here would be 'See how the use of italics help'.

should you use UK or US style?

The problem here is not in the text you are writing for UK or US audiences. You'd typically use the UK style for the former and the US style for the latter. But what do you do when you're writing for a global organisation? Especially one that uses English as its global language? Most of them select a style and promote that. For example, the Swiss-based company ABB, which also has a strong Swedish heritage, uses English throughout the world, with US spelling. Campbell Biscuits Europe, owned by the US-based Campbell Soup Company, uses US spelling. I've seen US-owned PR firm Burson-Marsteller use UK spelling in its London-originated documents and US spelling in those that come out of The Hague.

What's a billion? In the United States it's a thousand million. In the United Kingdom, it is traditionally a million million, although the US style seems to have gained acceptance. But you'll still sometimes see a government budget expressed in the United Kingdom from one source as a thousand million pounds and from another as a billion pounds. In fact, I've never seen a billion used in the United Kingdom to mean a million million except in explanations like this!

Pick a national style and stick with it. Use the colorful US spelling or the equally colourful British spelling, as appropriate, but not both. Your organization should have style. Or maybe your organisation should.

avoid sexism

These days it is bad form to talk about he or him when generalising about people. This creates the need to go awkward unless you are careful. As he or she will appreciate. I personally hate she/he or he/she. Or (s)he. Yecch!

If you write in the personal style, you can avoid it (much better than 'he or she can avoid it'). If being impersonal, try pluralising, which gives us the luxury of *they*. 'Readers will get more out of it. Yes, they will.' Much better than: 'The reader will get more out of it. Yes, he or she will.' Or, 'Yes, she/he will'. Or, 'Yes, (s)he will'.

There is a trend to use 'they' or 'them' in singular applications, which seems to be becoming an acceptable solution to this problem: 'The reader will get more out of it. Yes, they will.' It's not really legal, but you might get away with it.

take care when writing for the global audience

Since English is the language of business throughout the world, you may often find you are writing something that will be read by people for whom English is not the mother tongue. This raises the need to use easily recognisable expressions rather than idioms or slang.

Imagine the kinds of problems faced by someone who understands English quite well, but who has never lived in an English-speaking country, when confronted with something like this (which combines UK and US styles for further effect):

> Our bigwig was less than enchanted with the way our dog and pony show bombed and now seems to want to wash his hands of the whole ball of wax. He said he had thought that the big cheese at the client was crazy like a fox, which is why he ran the big idea, the one that was just off the vine, up the flagpole, quick as a flash. Bob's your uncle, he thought, as he waited for the salute. But it turned out to be a Catch-22 situation. It was a real red herring, in fact. An accident waiting to happen, you know?

That was an exaggerated example, but it should make the point that mother-tongue English is a minefield if you aren't mindful of the reader's mindset. Mind how you go. Do you mind?

In other words, don't outdrive your headlights. Give plenty of elbow room to your readers when it's showtime – more than just a blinding glimpse of the issues.

some rules when writing for this audience

- ■ Avoid using idioms and metaphors.
- ■ If you must use one, put it in quotes and explain it in parentheses, as below.
- ■ When you have finished the first draft, 'put on a different hat' (take the other person's point of view) and read it literally, as if you just barely understand English.
- ■ Ideally, ask one or two non-mother-tongue people in your target audience to read the text and give you their comments.

■ Failing their availability, try it out on a reasonably literate 10-year old – people learn English in much the same way as children.

use the right tone of voice

You can tell a lot about what a person means by their tone of voice. Is it authoritarian and threatening, like a mother calling to her errant son who is about to decapitate her best tulips: '*Justin*! Don't you *dare*!'? Is it pleading and grovelly? 'I really hope you'll like this. I tried my best.' Is it assertive? 'We're going to take that hill, and we'll take no prisoners!' Is it friendly? 'I'm really happy you agreed to join us.'

The tone of voice of your writing is something you should think about. For this book, I'd say the tone of voice is warm, encouraging and authoritative. That's what I intend, anyway.

the need to write for specific assignments

Business writing is about communicating to meet certain objectives. We listed the basic purposes of communication on page 1. These were identified as:

- to inform;
- to deliver news;
- to understand;
- to persuade;

- to reassure;
- to teach;
- to explain;
- to transact.

We took a closer look at these purposes on pages 14–22. We also listed the basic *methods* of communication on page 14. These were identified as:

- advertisement;
- article;
- backgrounder;
- book;
- brochure;

- catalogue;
- CV/resumé;
- e-mail;
- letter;
- manual;

- multimedia;
- newsletter;
- notice board;
- press release;
- proposal;
- Q&A/FAQs;

- sign;
- slides;
- speech;
- task description;
- video script;
- Web site.

This chapter takes a closer look at these methods in the sequence shown above, starting with five ways of writing advertising. I've added at the end of this chapter the assignment of writing a CV, in case you need one. Each method, where relevant, is accompanied by a checklist to help you get going.

creating advertising

The purposes of an advertisement may be:

- to make an announcement;
- to set the stage for something, build awareness;
- to build demand;
- to create or modify a brand or corporate image;
- to call the reader to some action, eg:
  - fill in a coupon, send for something;
  - make a phone call, ask for something;
  - visit a location (eg, a shop, theatre, bar, etc);
  - do something (eg, get a TV licence);
  - don't do something (eg, smoke).

There are many ways of advertising, including book-match covers, calendars, bus cards, skywriting and sandwich boards. This book looks very briefly at the more traditional methods:

- print advertising;
- outdoor poster advertising;
- TV advertising;

▓ radio advertising;
▓ direct mail advertising.

checklist for creating an advertisement

If you use this basic checklist, you will find it much easier to create an advertisement:

▓ Audience:
 – Who;
 – Where?
▓ What is the advertisement for (eg, what product or service)?
▓ What is the key message?
▓ What do you want the audience to do, think or feel as a result of this advertisement?
▓ What are the key features of the subject?
▓ What are the key benefits of the subject?
▓ What's special or unique about it?
▓ What must be included in the advertisement?
▓ What must not be included in the advertisement?
▓ What are the time constraints (eg, Easter, summer, year-end, etc)?
▓ Intended medium (eg, print, TV, radio, etc)?
▓ Must this advertisement respect any other communications (eg, other ads, media stories, corporate identity, Web site, etc)?
▓ Remarks?

writing a print display advertisement

The components of a print display advertisement are typically:

▓ headline;

▦ sub-head;
▦ cross-heads;
▦ body copy;
▦ message;
▦ illustration(s);
▦ logo;
▦ coupon or response device.

headline

The headline is there to attract attention and transmit a hint of the key concept, so that your *prospect* will be provoked to stop and read more of the ad. If they don't read on, they will at least get enough of the idea to be left with a positive perception. The headline must work with the overall ad layout and any illustration to accomplish this.

Advertising genius David Ogilvy, in his book *Ogilvy on Advertising*, says that on average, five times as many people read the headline as the body copy. 'Unless your headline sells your product, you have wasted 90 per cent of your money,' he suggests. You want the ones who do read the whole ad to be your prospects and not just passers-by.

According to Starch, the advertising research company, consumers are exposed to 623 advertising impressions every day, of which they only remember nine favourably one day later. That means 69 out of 70 messages are wasted. And it means you have quite a challenge in writing an effective headline.

My personal test of a good headline is to read it and say 'so what?' If the answer is 'who cares?' or 'so, nothing' the headline doesn't work. Ideally, a headline should promise the reader a benefit or deliver some news, or both.

'Now you can get to Gatwick Airport from Central London in 30 minutes'

sub-head

The advertising sub-head works with the headline to beckon the reader on. It's like the subtitle of a book (see page 26). It should lead the reader into the body copy. See how the headline and sub-head work together here:

'How to take out STAINS
– Use Rinso and follow these easy directions'

Sometimes you will see the opposite of a sub-head (a super-head?), which runs above the headline. This is known as the eyebrow. It might amplify the address of the message:

'For everyone thinking of buying a new car'

cross-head

This is the heading above various chunks of copy and works like sub-heads do in any text, to help the reader navigate through the piece – see page 29.

body copy

This is the main text that delivers your message. It should be logically presented, with a beginning, middle and end. It must hold the reader's interest all the way through. A good model of content is:

- ■ problem or context statement:
  - – this might have been established with the headline, sub-head or illustration;
- ■ your solution;
- ■ discussion, reinforcing the solution, stating benefits and your unique selling proposition;
- ■ conclusion – what to do next, the call to action.

message

The message doesn't occupy a dedicated place in the ad, with the cross-head 'Message' above it. It is the overall takeaway from the ad – what the ad is saying. It comes through from the combination of the ad's ingredients.

illustration(s)

Some ads don't contain an illustration at all, but on the premise that a picture can be very effective, you'll find that an illustration will help a lot in conveying your message.

Some brands' images are so powerful, the illustration does it all. Think of the campaigns (in the United Kingdom) for Silk Cut or Benson & Hedges Gold cigarettes. They typically don't even run the logo or brand name in their ads. Maybe it's guilt?

Illustrations are like pictorial headlines. They are there to provoke interest as well as help tell the story.

logo

The logo is the signature of the ad. Some logos are so well known you can look at just the visual symbol and get the brand name, for example the Mercedes Benz three-pointed star, or the Nike swoosh.

Very often, adjacent to the logo is what I call the slogo (the slogan by the logo). This is the little saying that also forms part of the signature, as in 'British Airways – The world's favourite airline'.

coupon or response device

If you want the reader to take a specific action, such as phone for or send for a brochure, the best way to induce this is to run a coupon – even if you just want them to phone.

Don't forget to put the Web site address on the ad, in a type size that can be read without a microscope.

writing a poster advertisement

Outdoor posters or billboards are mostly viewed by people in transit and therefore need minimum copy – basically just a headline. An exception is billboards at such locations as railway or underground stations where people often have plenty of reading time as they await their trains.

The straightforward outdoor poster needs a dramatic illustration or art treatment, because a lot of the message will be conveyed with this. The copy should be no more than 6 to 10 words. This is really reminder advertising.

The transportation poster can have much longer copy, so the comments made for print advertising apply (see page 64).

writing a TV advertisement

TV commercials are highly specialised and often cost hundreds of thousand of pounds to produce, and even more to run, especially in prime time. I don't intend to cover conventional TV advertisements here – that's another whole book. But you may be called upon to write a simple 'talking head' spot, so then what?

You have a very limited amount of time, probably 10, 20, 30, 40 or 60 seconds. You can only convey a small amount of information, so confine your message to just one or two points. What visuals can you use to help tell your story? TV is a visual medium, so let appropriate images work for you. You also have sound, so anything that can be recorded can be incorporated – a lunch whistle, a jet flying over, a machine gun, an explosion, a police siren, a ringing telephone, music, office or factory sounds, a baby crying, a thunderstorm, and so on.

As usual, you need an opening that will provoke the viewer's attention now. There's no time for them to turn their head – they'll miss it. So start with a relevant attention grabber, give your message and end with your call to action. If that is for the viewer to make a phone call, repeat the phone number and display it on the screen for as long as possible.

script approval

You may well find that the commercial must be approved by a regulatory body, such as the Broadcast Advertising Clearance Centre and/or the station running it before it can be run. Check with the TV station involved. If so, it makes sense to get approval of the script prior to producing the commercial.

script format

Most TV commercials are storyboarded. This means that each visual element is depicted on a mini representation of a TV screen and beneath each screen appears the copy that relates to that visual element. Storyboards are used to develop the production elements (set design, integration of visuals and approximate blocking of the scenes, etc). They are also used to obtain approvals and for archival purposes.

A storyboard shows maybe nine screens on an A4 page. Here's a bit of one (VO means 'voice-over') in Figure 4.1.

VO: Ever since   baby was on   she hasn't smoked
Mummy knew   the way.   a cigarette.

Figure 4.1 *Sample TV commercial storyboard*

A TV commercial is also originated as a shooting script, to a fairly standard format, something like this:

Table 4.1 *Sample shooting script*

Vision	Sound
camera and activity instructions go here, such as:	words and sounds go here, such as:
open on wide shot of professional office, presenter at desk on telephone, listening. He speaks, then hangs up	SFX: busy office noises Presenter (on phone): Right: We'll have the first draft to you Tuesday at noon
cut to close up, presenter looking into camera	Presenter (to camera): More new business! It's almost more than I can handle!
etc, etc	etc, etc

writing a radio advertisement

Unlike the visual media, radio enables you to create images in the listener's mind. Want to have a cowboy riding the Concorde bareback at Mach 2? You can. Want to take the listener to the Casbah, or Red Square, or the bottom of the Pacific Ocean? You can – and all in the same 30 seconds if you like. The problem is you can't *show* anything visually, like a phone number or an address. You have to conjure it up.

The most important thing to keep in mind is that radio is a background medium. People tend to have the radio on while they are doing something else, especially driving, reading or working, so it is unlikely the listener is giving their full attention to it. Hence your commercial must change their listening priority from background to foreground.

content

A good model of content is:

▨ attention-getting opening;
▨ problem or context statement;
▨ your solution, stating benefits and your unique selling proposition;
▨ conclusion – what to do next, the call to action.

Since stations tend to cluster commercials in batches, you need to start with a device that not only attracts attention but also indicates this is a new spot. Avoid sounding like everyone else. For example, many stations tend to run a lot of commercials for various mobile phone and computer stores. These all tend to sound the same, and are hard to distinguish one from the other. So listen to the station(s) you'll be using and get a feel for the sound of their commercials, then see how you can differentiate your own spot.

A very good technique is to employ humour. If you can afford it, use established comedians. They will help with, or take over, the writing. If the humour is great, the listener will shift you to the foreground of their attention. They may not catch it all the first time the spot is aired, but they'll make a mental note to listen the next time it runs.

Many local radio stations will offer to write the commercial for you. Certainly you should take advantage of their expertise and work in cooperation with each other.

approvals

As with television advertising, the script for a radio commercial will most likely have to be approved before use by a body such as the Broadcast Advertising Clearance Centre. Check with the radio station.

script format

Here is a typical radio commercial script, written by my brother, Richard Foster, who creates advertising at the agency Abbott Mead Vickers • BBDO (used with permission):

<u>Health Education Authority</u>
Anti smoking   40 seconds   'Will Powder'

SFX: *Shop doorbell*
John Cleese: Ah, good morning, I'd like some will powder please.
Chemist: What's that, sir, like foot powder is it?
John Cleese: Beg your pardon?
Chemist: Is it like foot powder?
John Cleese: Well, you're the chemist, you tell me. It's for giving up smoking. My wife says nicotine patches and chewing gum are alright, but what you really need is some will powder.
Chemist: Ah, I think you may have misheard her, sir.
John Cleese: Pardon?
Chemist (louder): I think she meant will *power*, sir.
John Cleese: Oh, the American film actor. Has he given up smoking?

Chemist: I tell you what, sir, try some of this. It's for removing earwax.
John Cleese: Earwigs? I want to give up smoking.
Chemist: Well why don't you just stop?
John Cleese: Er... a quarter to four.
MVO: If you want to give up smoking, the Quitline can help. Call 0171 487 3000.

making broadcast advertising work better

Drayton Bird, in his book *Commonsense Direct Marketing* (Kogan Page), offers these suggestions for making your broadcast commercials more effective:

▨ Are you really exploiting the medium? For instance, if you're on TV, is it truly visual, or just words set to pictures? If you're on radio, is it just words or are you using the medium properly to conjure up images in people's minds?
▨ Is there a key visual or sound that acts as a mnemonic device to fix it in the memory. Have you repeated it?
▨ Is the product the hero – or is it the execution?
▨ If there's music, is it relevant or just gloss? The same applies to any visual device. Everything should be essential to making the commercial work better.
▨ Do you get straight to the point? You have limited time: get people involved instantly. In particular, a dramatic opening at the beginning of radio commercials to set them aside from the tapestry of sound – a loud noise or a fanfare are obvious things. A challenging statement is another, or some tricky form of delivery like a person speaking very fast.
▨ Does the product or service solve a problem? If so, is it shown clearly?
▨ If you are seeking a response, have you made it clear? Preferably at the beginning, so people know they have to take note of where to reply.

writing a direct mail letter

This is what is known, unkindly, as 'junk mail'. We all receive it. Do you open yours? If you don't I suggest you do, if only to see how the pros are doing it these days.

relevant direct mail can be memorable

A recent issue of *Marketing* magazine quoted some interesting research. As mentioned earlier, according to the US research company Starch, consumers are exposed to 623 advertising impressions every day, of which they only remember nine favourably a day later. Yet a mailing to a file of frequent flyers was recalled by 74 per cent of them after three months. This type of impact was confirmed by a mailing on cosmetics to another relevant audience, where 70 per cent recalled it after three months.

The list is all important. And so is the relevance of the message to the audience. Think of your dearest hobby or pastime. Now imagine a really interesting piece of news about it that was mailed to you cold – would you feel responsive? Probably. It's that type of impact you should be striving for in any mailing you do.

So the most important thing in direct mail, after making sure the letter goes to the right person, is to get them to open the envelope.

Some years ago, in the United States, I wanted to run a communication with the owners of Mooney aeroplanes – private four-seater 'aerial Ferraris'. Since aircraft ownership is all recorded, coming up with a list of the 4,500 people involved was easy. But how could we get them to open the envelope? Well, every Mooney owner knows who Roy LoPresti is – the man who revolutionised the design of the Mooney a few years ago, and made it fly faster and smoother than ever before. So on the envelope, we put a slanting headline 'Here's news about Mooney from Roy LoPresti.' Roy signed the letter inside. We offered, among other things, a video brochure on the new Mooneys for $30. We sold 650 tapes – a 14 per cent response! And three $120,000 aeroplanes were sold, directly attributable to the mailing.

Direct mail is the most measurable and testable advertising medium there is. You can try different approaches, track responses and see which works best.

content

As with all other advertising media, you have to get the reader's attention after you've got them to open the envelope. The mailing piece will no doubt consist of various components, for example:

- ▧ outside envelope with teaser to encourage opening;
- ▧ covering letter;
- ▧ brochure or colourful pamphlet describing offer in detail;
- ▧ some other item to maintain interest and curiosity;
- ▧ response device.

Always be mindful of mailing costs, so aim to keep the weight down. Keep checking the weight as you design the package. A few grams too many can cost you a fortune in extra postage.

the letter

'The letter is the key element in direct mail,' says Drayton Bird in *Commonsense Direct Marketing*. 'It comments, amplifies, makes more human, sells the facts in the other material.'

If possible personalise it – easy to do with sophisticated mailing lists and computers. But make sure you don't end up with a disaster like 'Dear Mr AMMechE, BSc', which is what happened when a not very smart computer program tried to personalise 'J Stephens AMMechE, BSc'.

Writing a direct mail letter, like any other communication, requires you to put yourself in the mindset of the reader. What would make you want to read it? A good model of content for a covering letter is:

- relevant introductory headline;
- personalised salutation;
- attention-getting opening paragraph that sets the scene for your proposition;
- your offer, stating benefits and your unique selling proposition;
- one or two case histories or independent third party endorsement to support the idea;
- reference to other components included in the mailing ('see the accompanying brochure for more details');
- conclusion – what to do next, the call to action.

response devices

The easier it is for them to reply, the better a reply rate you will have. Try putting a fax form on the back of your letter, inviting instant response. They just have to fill in a few blanks and tick a couple of boxes. This works very effectively.

Or you may want the respondent to make a phone call. If you can, make it a toll-free number (0800) or (0500) in the United Kingdom (800) in the United States and Canada.

You can also do postage-free reply envelopes or use a 'Freepost' address that lets the respondent reply at no charge using their own stationery.

writing articles for the print media

The subject of writing articles is broad enough to merit a book in itself. Since it only merits a segment here, let's take the point of view that you want to write an article about some aspect of what your organisation does. The purpose in writing such an article is to further your cause, to give background to an activity or to support other communication activities.

Writing an article is a very good way to build credibility and develop interest. You can use the technique to establish yourself (or whoever's name bylines the story) as an authority on a subject.

where to start

There are two choices for starting points: you have an interesting story; you want to place an article in a certain publication.

If you start with the idea of an interesting story, where would you like to see it run? Who do you want to tell the story to? What publications do they read? Which leads to the second starting point, placing an article in a certain publication. In fact, it all boils down to the need to...

understand the angle of a story

You can tell the same story several times over to different audiences if you understand the concept of the *angle* or *slant* of the story. It involves knowing what the medium is looking for in communicating to its audiences.

There are two broad categories of business publications, horizontal and vertical:

- ▓ horizontal – those that cover several industries, perhaps from one point of view, eg:
  - *Marketing*;
  - *Financial Times*;
  - *The Economist*;
  - *Business Week International*;
  - *Fortune International*;

▨ vertical – titles about the same industry, eg:
- *Television Week*;
- *TV Producer*;
- *Broadcast*.

Say you want to write an article to publicise a book about public relations. The story aimed at readers of a trade magazine such as *The Bookseller* would be about the book's marketing, and would discuss how the book fits in with other titles in the category – business books. The story aimed at readers of *PR Week* would talk about the author's experience in PR and give information about its content and what the book is intended to do. The story for the *Your Own Business* column in *The Times*, would talk about how small businesses and independent people may have had trouble getting publicity and now there's a new book aimed at helping them overcome this barrier.

If you're aiming a story at several different publications in one vertical category, come up with a different angle for each.

know your context

It is important to present your message in the right context. You need to recognise what's going on around you and make the story relevant to reality. In fact, the reality of the world around you may very well be the impetus for the story. For example, a story about the PR book that reflects the market-place context might have language like this in it:

With the increasing tendency in the United Kingdom for people to be running their own businesses, there is a growing need for these people, often former managers within large organisations, to develop basic marketing-communications skills. One such skill is the art of generating publicity to promote a product, service or idea.

placement

Placing an article in an appropriate publication is not particularly difficult. You may want to have it bylined by your spokesperson, or by the managing director, or by the brand manager of the product. This provides them with a platform where they are seen to carry some clout on the subject. The secret of success in this area is to know your medium and know your journalists. If you have a good idea of what the publication covers, designing a story to appeal to its readers should not be hard.

When you have the concept, if you don't know who to call, send the editor a fax or e-mail saying something like: 'Would you be interested in an article about ____, written by ____, one of the foremost authorities on the subject? Please let me know to whom I should address this within your organisation.' Then follow up with a phone call a day later: 'It's about the fax I sent yesterday... ' This should result in a name. Then you contact the name and say: '(Editor) suggested I talk to you about... etc, etc'. This should at least result in an invitation to submit the article. Get the names of the personal assistants and secretaries as you speak to them and become their allies. Include them in the action: why the story is interesting, why the writer is special, how important it would be to have the story in the publication and so on. They will help you drive the story on to the pages of the publication.

using case histories

To bring your story to life, use case histories. These anecdotal items help to build credibility, because they are real world. Look at the case histories on pages 74 and 135, for example.

Case histories lead naturally to quotes from people, These also make the story resonate with solid information. See page 65 for an example, quoting adman David Ogilvy.

do some research

One of the best ways to drive a story is to do some research and then publish the findings. The media love headlines like:

'Eighty per cent of 12-year-olds can't spell aquarium'

Here's an exercise. Take today's newspaper and go through it looking for stories that are driven by research. Here's what was found in *The Times* on one day recently:

■ 'High Street sales fall in October' (the latest survey from the Confederation of British Industry shows...);
■ 'EC jobless up' (according to Eurostat, the EC statistics office...);
■ 'Private consultants are relying on public sector work to stay afloat in recession' (in its latest survey of chief executives, the Management Consultancies Association...);
■ 'Crisis? What crisis?' (according to a recent Gallup poll, over two-thirds of middle-aged men believe the mid-life...).

If you want a headline about what you want to promote in your story, what is the research *you* have to do to generate it?

To promote the publicity book, we might want a headline that says something like:

'Seventy-two per cent of small business owners believe they frequently miss out on publicity opportunities'

Now what's the research we have to do to drive that headline (given that we'd use the actual percentage, rather than the made up figure in the example)?

Somehow we should do a survey of small business owners to find out their attitudes towards publicity. One of the questions might be: Do you feel you never/sometimes/frequently miss out on publicity opportunities? Yes. Research is a valuable tool to get a story going.

checklist for writing an article

These are suggested headings for a pre-articular checklist. Use the items that seem relevant to your task:

- Working title?
- Subtitle?
- Byline (who is the 'author')?
- Deadline (when must it be finished by)?
- Desired audience?
- Target publication(s)?
- Key message (what do you want the audience to understand after reading this)?
- Other pertinent considerations/factors:
  - Who?
  - Who is this about?
  - Who did it?
  - Who started it?
  - Who is involved?
  - Who is in charge?
  - Who wants it?
  - Who needs it?
  - Who wins?
  - Who loses?
  - Who is threatened?
  - Who should not be involved?
  - Who knows about this?
  - Who can be interviewed?
  - Who can be quoted?
  - Who else?

■ What?
  - What is it?
  - What was it?
  - What was it supposed to be?
  - What is it about?
  - What does it do?
  - What could it be?
  - What is similar?
  - What's unique or special about it?
  - What else?
■ When?
  - When did it happen?
  - When was it finalised?
  - When was it made?
  - When was it first used?
  - When will it happen?
  - When is it ready?
  - When else?
■ Where?
  - Where did it happen?
  - Where is it built?
  - Where is it used?
  - Where can you see it?
  - Where can you get it?
  - Where is it going?
  - Where else?
■ Why?
  - Why was it done?
  - Why not?
  - Why should anyone... ?
  - Why is it needed?
  - Why must we... ?
  - Why else?
■ How?
  - How does it work?
  - How do you get one?

- How big?
- How far?
- How much?
- How else?

writing a backgrounder

A backgrounder often accompanies a press release (see page 106), but has a longer shelf life. It's a story/article that goes into the subject in some depth. Its purpose is, as its name suggests, to give background to the message.

A backgrounder on the publicity book would go into the need for a manual on getting publicity and would distinguish it from other books on the market, for example its own strategy of practising what it preaches. It would go into examples of this in more detail. It would talk about the audience and their current economic environment. It might quote several people – for example one or two potential readers on why they have a need for publicity and the difficulty they have in knowing how to go about getting it.

A typical backgrounder might run for up to six pages of double-spaced type. As always, it must be dated and give contact names and numbers.

checklist for writing a backgrounder

Use the article writing checklist (see page 81).

writing a book

I do a stand-up piece at seminars called: 'Write a book about what you do'. It is absolutely the best way to become an acknowledged leader in your area whom people seek out for advice!

check the existing literature

Look at your line of business. What books are there out there now on the subject? You should have a reasonable awareness of this, but if you don't, visit a good library. Go to a couple of good bookshops and check out the scene.

checklist for writing a book

To start, answer these questions:

- ■ What is my objective?
- ■ What is the working title?
- ■ What is the subtitle?
- ■ What is the book about?
- ■ Who will buy it?
- ■ What needs does it fill?
- ■ What does the author bring to the party?
- ■ What is the format (hardcover, paperback, etc)?
- ■ Who should publish it?

Assuming you can answer these, start working. Write the table of contents. Write single paragraph descriptions of each chapter, and write at least one chapter.

selling your book

Forget agents. They are mostly useless for this kind of work. I've never had an agent able to sell a trade book on my behalf. Most of them don't even want to look at what you do, because they're 'too busy'. Yet I've sold over 20 books on my own, working directly with publishers.

So write to your target publisher. If you don't know who to contact, telephone and ask for the name of the person to write to, and send a one-page descriptive letter, with this information:

■ the proposed title;
■ the target audience;
■ the rationale/need for the book;
■ the chapter headings;
■ how many pages you expect it to be;
■ the style – paperback, coffee table, etc;
■ how many illustrations;
■ when and how you can deliver it (floppy disk, paper, etc);
■ your price ideas;
■ your timetable;
■ your credentials as author – CV, copies of articles, etc.

You may not make a lot of money writing a book, but the mileage you can get out of it is worth all the aggro.

writing a brochure

A brochure is an alternative to reality. It is the equivalent of the free taste you get in a good cheese shop. It provides a continuity from the moment of contact to the moment of taking on the proposition. So it represents the product or service until it has been acquired or employed. It must reassure the target that this will be good. It must describe the benefits (see page 16) in glowing terms, creating desire. It must impart some of the same feelings as the real thing in an appetising way. It must ring of the same quality as the end product. It must inform and be a reference point (including the provision of things like technical specifications, dimensions, addresses, phone and fax numbers, and so on).

When your target wants to take action, the brochure must make it easy to get to a successful conclusion (business!). Ideally, it should then become a hand-me-down, finding its way as an unsolicited testimonial into the hands of one of your targets' friends, perhaps with a recommendation to use the subject matter.

Brochure copy, like everything else, should be written with your target audience's interests in mind, not your client's. Not, 'We offer the finest tyres', but, 'If you seek the finest tyres, you'll find them here... '. Use a compelling statement as a key opening headline: 'One call gets all your ribbons, diskettes, paper and supplies delivered FREE overnight and saves you up to 71 per cent!' – that's from a mail order catalogue for Viking Direct. Much more motivational than: 'Your number-one office supplies house'.

If the brochure is intended to be informative and educational, give it an appropriate title, eg: 'The Royal Mail Guide to Successful Direct Mail' or 'Make Communications Make a Difference' (from BT).

checklist for writing a brochure

- ■ What is the product or service?
- ■ Who is the brochure aimed at?
- ■ What is its purpose?
- ■ Title?
- ■ Subtitle?
- ■ Is this an update of an existing item?
- ■ Who is the expert?
- ■ Deadline?
- ■ How will it be distributed?
- ■ What will be its shelf life?
- ■ What illustrations are needed:
  - – drawings ☐ new ☐ existing;
  - – diagrams ☐ new ☐ existing;
  - – charts ☐ new ☐ existing;
  - – maps ☐ new ☐ existing;
  - – other ☐ new ☐ existing.
- ■ What contact points should be listed?

▨ Available budget (this impacts design, etc)?
▨ Must it conform to other materials?
▨ What about the Web site?

writing a catalogue

I'm making the assumption that your catalogue will be used to order goods. So it's a bit like a menu in a restaurant. It needs to be well organised and appetising. But there's no waiter hovering to answer questions, so it must be crystal clear.

Catalogue copywriting is the traditional training ground for wannabe advertising copywriters. You learn to write to a specific, tight space requirement and how to write tersely yet persuasively.

Take a look at a selection of mail order catalogues for inspiration. One of the best is that of Viking Direct (0800) 424444 – 'Your favourite office products for less – overnight!' It now has a mind-blowing feature. On the inside-front cover of the one a friend just received is a printed notice:

This catalogue belongs to:
Jonathan Wheeling
Since your first order with Viking on March 3 1995,
these are the office supplies you've ordered most.
You may find this handy when you need to check your supplies.

... then it lists some items he uses and tells him the stock number and page number of each one. Talk about listening to and getting close to your customer!

On the front cover of the Viking catalogue, as well as the blurbs about the special offers inside and a reiteration of its USPs (unique selling propositions), like a one-year guarantee and *overnight* free delivery ('even on small orders of £30 or more'), it gives the page numbers for the index and order forms, and its phone numbers, all toll-free, even its fax order line. Viking makes it easy and a pleasure to deal with.

Catalogue producers realise they are in a numbers game. They basically have a target income per page, based upon their operating, production and distribution costs. This means that the amount of space available for an item is related to the amount of revenue it should generate. So low-cost, low-profit items get small space. High-cost, high-profit items get much more – maybe even a page or a spread.

Drayton Bird, in *Commonsense Direct Marketing*, offers these suggestions for improving your catalogue:

▥ Find a way to make your catalogue different.
▥ Make your catalogue personal, eg, with an introductory letter (see Viking item, above).
▥ Remember the cover is your prime selling spot.
▥ Keep in mind that space is at a premium.
▥ Don't underestimate how many items you can get on a page.
▥ Create changes of pace and interest.
▥ Make every entry a 'mini-ad', with its own headline.
▥ Use the same style for your catalogue as you would for other communications.
▥ Note that photographs usually, but not always, do better than illustrations.
  – For reasons of finance and logistics, it often pays to use as few photographers or illustrators as possible.
▥ Pay great attention to the order form and how it is planned.
▥ Take great care that captions and prices are easily related to items.
▥ Be aware that results can be boosted enormously (sometimes over 50 per cent) by the use of contests and sweepstakes.

checklist for writing a catalogue

▥ What is the product or service series?
▥ Who is the catalogue aimed at?
▥ Title?
▥ Subtitle?

▓ Is this an update of a previous catalogue?
▓ Deadline?
▓ Shelf life/Expiration date?
▓ How will it be distributed?
▓ Directory and index clearly located and flagged?
▓ Clear organisation into functional sections?
▓ Concise, persuasive product descriptions with visuals?
▓ Visuals and descriptions clearly linked and identified?
▓ Understandable, non-complex item coding:
  – easy variation handling (sizes, colours, quantities)?
▓ Detailed, clear prices?
▓ Simple, easy-to-find and use order form?
▓ Repeated display of telephone number for help or ordering?
▓ Available budget (this impacts design, etc)?
▓ Must it conform to other materials?
▓ What about the Web site?

writing e-mail

THE WORST THINGS ABOUT ELECTRONIC MAIL (E-MAIL) ARE SO OFTEN THE LACK OF FORMATTING AND THE 'ON-THE-RUN' NATURE OF THE MESSAGES SENT. YOU CAN END UP WITH TEXT THAT IS PRINTED IN ALL CAPITALS AND LAID OUT ON THE BASIS OF 80 CHARACTERS PER LINE (THIS TEXT IS ABOUT 50 PER LINE) WITH POOR PUNCTUATION, TERRIBLE SPELING AND NO WHITE SPACE. PART OF THE PROBLEM IS THAT THE SENDER THINKS TIME CAN BE SAVED WITH E-MAIL, SO THEY JUST BASH OUT ANY OLD DRIVEL ON THEIR KEYBOARD, WITHOUT THINKING ABOUT THE CHALLENGE THEY PRESENT TO THEIR POOR READER. E-MAIL SHOULD BE COMPOSED AS CARE-FULLY AS ANY COMMUNICATION. USE FORMATTING IF IT'S AVAILABLE AND INCLUDE WHITE SPACE.

There is so much unwanted e-mail floating around that many people start their day by deleting, unread, the e-mail they assume to be 'spam' (unsolicited junk messages). This means one of the big challenges facing the sender is making sure that their message is not instantly consigned to the cyberspace trash bin. Probably the most important skill in composing an e-mail message is coming up with a good subject line. Leaving it blank will produce a subject that says 'no subject'. Not very helpful. Write something specific, ideally slightly provocative, such as: WE NEED TO TALK, WHEN R U AVAILABLE? Putting the subject in BLOCK CAPS helps it stand out.

Then there's the reply. One of the useful features of e-mail is that you can arrange a reply to a message by simply clicking the 'Reply' button. But you need to deal with the subject. Let's say you receive the following message:

'Subject: GRANDVILLE PROJECT
'Jo:
'I like what you did with the Grandville project. Nice work!
'Did Mary brief you on the Humphrey project? If so, when will you have it finished? We need this ASAP!
'Harry'

Now if you simply click reply, the subject will come up as 'Re: GRANDVILLE PROJECT'. This is not very helpful if your message is:

'Harry:
'Mary never said anything about the Humphrey project and she's off on three week's holiday. What's it all about?
'Jo'

It would be much better if you change the subject to this:

'WHAT HUMPHREY PROJECT? – NO BRIEF RECEIVED'

A lot of people leave the previous message, in its entirety, as part of their reply. In fact, this can happen again and again. So an ongoing correspondence can contain a lot of extraneous material that clogs up bandwidth and disk space and slows everything down. It's smarter to delete unwanted text – only including relevant content in the reply.

using emoticons

Since e-mail is not face to face, a lot of people use emoticons to express feelings with their informal messages. These are little images made from the characters on your keyboard. They typically look like a face (eyes, nose and mouth) when rotated 90° clockwise. The most prevalent are :) denoting a smile and : (denoting a frown. Here are some more:

:]	significant happiness (big grin)
:[	unhappiness (stiff upper lip)
: C	significant unhappiness
:/	or :\ undecided
: D	laughing out loud
;)	winking
; D	laughing/winking

You can have some fun making up your own.

using acronyms

FYI e-mail is so fast, SH acronyms often work well, IMHO. BYKT. Here are some of the most prevalent 4 U, BTW. Remember, only use these in an informal context.

2	to
4	for
ASAP	as soon as possible
BFN	bye for now
BTW	by the way

BYKT	but you knew that
CMIIW	correct me if I'm wrong
EOL	end of lecture
FAQ	frequently asked question(s)
FITB	fill in the blanks
FWIW	for what it's worth
FYI	for your information
HTH	hope this helps
IAC	in any case
IAE	in any event
IMHO	in my humble opinion
IOW	in other words
LOL	laughing out loud
MHOTY	my hat's off to you
NRN	no reply necessary
OIC	oh, I see
OTOH	on the other hand
ROF	rolling on the floor
RSN	real soon now
SH	shorthand
SITD	still in the dark
TIA	thanks in advance
TIC	tongue in cheek
TTYL	talk to you later
TYVM	thank you very much
U	you

writing a letter or memorandum

The distinction between a letter and a memo is that a letter is usually an external communication, while a memo is an internal one. If it starts 'Dear Harry', it's a letter. If it starts 'From: (Name) To: (Name)', it's a memo. Letters observe little courtesies you won't find in memos, such as a closing salutation like 'yours sincerely'.

Aim to confine your letters and memos to one or, at the most, two pages, if possible. Use a subject heading. State the purpose of the communiqué in the first paragraph. Present the message in a logical sequence. Use sub-heads if it is lengthy. Close with a call to action, expectation or next step. Gauge the tone to the formality of the message and the basis of your relationship with the reader. But obey the Plain English Code (see page 6).

Make sure the letter or memo is dated clearly. If you're referring to other correspondence, use that item's date and subject to identify it: 'In response to your letter to me of June 16 2002 about road testing the Skoda... '.

If the item is being circulated to several people, show all their names as addressees or as those receiving a copy (you'll often see the abbreviation 'cc' which means 'carbon copy' even though hardly anyone uses carbon paper anymore. You may also see 'c', meaning 'copy'. If it is a large list receiving a memo, you can say 'To: see distribution list' then append a list in an appropriate place. If you want someone to read the letter, but it is not essential that the addressee knows this, you can send a 'blind copy' ('bcc') to the secret person. I smell politics!

if you are faxing it...

It's a good idea to mail a hard copy as confirmation if you send it initially by fax. Also phone shortly after you fax it to make sure it arrived and is clear. Never assume that it got through just because you sent it. Sending a fax does not mean receiving a fax. I once sent one to a client on a tight deadline on a weekend. After three hours he hadn't called back with his comments, so I phoned him. He said 'Where the hell is it? I've been waiting!'. It turned out I had the wrong number. What's even worse is that the wrong number was also a fax, and on the following Monday I got a fax from some mystery company wondering what this strange fax was all about.

checklist for writing a letter or memo

- ■ Who is it going to:
  - – prime addressee(s);
  - – copies;
  - – blind copies?
- ■ Who is it from?
- ■ Is there a deadline by which it must be delivered?
- ■ Title/subject?
- ■ Purpose of communication?
- ■ Background/context/situation?
- ■ Key facts?
- ■ Questions being asked?
- ■ Conclusion?
- ■ What do you want the addressee to do as a result?
- ■ What other correspondence/documents are involved:
  - – subject;
  - – from/to;
  - – date?
- ■ Must it be approved by anyone before being mailed?
- ■ Must anything be included (eg a brochure, a form, a copy of something)?
- ■ What about e-mail (see page 89)?

writing a manual

What I mean by a manual is a reference source book, such as you might have with a set of computer software. Its purpose is to tell the user how to do or operate something. Hence I suggest you don't use a typical software manual as your inspiration. They are usually terrible!

PDF files

A lot of manuals are now distributed over the Web as downloadable PDF (portable document format) files. These require the reader to use Adobe Acrobat software (which can be downloaded free from the Web) to read or print them. The PDF method cuts down on your printing and distribution costs, and allows the document to be kept up to date easily.

manual content and checklist

The components of a 'how to' manual are:

▓ Detailed description of what the manual refers to:
  - date of issue;
  - previous manuals now superseded by this one;
  - reference number of subject (eg Claris Works 2.2).
▓ If the manual is loose-leaf and subject to amendment, a list of amendments included and space to log future changes.
▓ If it is a user manual for some gadget, such as a camera or stereo, very clear diagram(s) up front identifying parts labelled using key numbers and call-outs. Make sure that all references to components always use exactly the same terminology as depicted on the diagram (eg, don't call it 'shutter release' in one paragraph and 'trigger' in another. Use the diagram reference number every time, if relevant, eg: 'shutter release [7]'.)
▓ Sections or chapters in logical sequence. If possible, tab or colour code each section.
▓ Typical content structure:
  - table of contents: very clear and detailed so that it cannot be missed;
  - 'read this first' section (for absolutely crucial information): flag this section on the front cover;
  - 'how to use this manual' section: use visual flow chart if possible;

- minimum requirements: what you must have to be able to use this (eg, Macintosh computer using System 7 or higher, 8 Mb RAM, at least 40 Mb hard disk space);
- 'getting started' section;
- application discussion sections in logical sequence: illustrated with diagrams, sample screens, etc;
- glossary of terms, if needed;
- troubleshooting guide;
- contact points for more information;
- very comprehensive index;
- user-registration card, to notify publisher of where to send amendments or other important advice;
- pocket-sized quick-reference card, showing key actions.

writing for interactive multimedia

Interactive, here, means the ability to access and travel through the content of a multimedia information resource on your own terms, going in the direction you want to go, looking at the information you want to look at, in a sequence of your own choosing. Multimedia can be a combination of still images and graphics, text, computer animation, live-action moving pictures and sound.

uses of multimedia

There are basically three key applications for multimedia:

■ training and education, eg:
   - A-level chemistry;
   - speaking French;

- using your new computer;
- understanding Microsoft Word;
■ reference, eg:
- an encyclopedia;
- a museum guide;
- maintenance procedures and parts descriptions for a Ford Mondeo;
■ marketing, eg:
- point-of-sale kiosks at a travel agency;
- trade-show presentations;
- CD ROMs for individual use (for example to give facts on and demonstrate a new car);
- Internet.

benefits of multimedia

■ clear, cogent and consistent messages;
■ personalised presentation or learning environment;
■ orderly, open and efficient information flow;
■ additional support for the teaching, training, information or marketing professional;
■ information or instruction available at a convenient time and place to meet a variety of needs;
■ non-judgemental, non-threatening dialogue and immediate feedback;
■ active participation and demonstration;
■ safety in otherwise hazardous demonstrations, eg: fire drills and procedures;
■ ongoing lifelong learning or self-enhancement;
■ motivation.

technical background

The multimedia content is most often delivered these days on an electronic screen, controlled through a keyboard and a mouse, or sometimes via a touch-sensitive screen, and sourced from a CD ROM (compact disk – read-only memory: used with computers) or CD-I (compact disk – interactive: used with TVs). It can also be sourced from a hard disk and, of course, the Internet or other online resource over a telephone line.

digital vs analogue

Because the information is stored on the disk in digital form, it can be accessed at any point in a second or two. Compare this with an audiotape cassette with 12 songs on it. To hear song number nine, you have to fast-forward the tape three-quarters of the way through – a process that can take a minute or more. A tape stores its information in linear (analogue) form.

content media analysis

In the early stages, you need to analyse the messages you want to deliver and determine how to do this. So start with an outline of the content story. Then determine how best you can tell this story. Bear in mind any materials that might already exist, such as videos, diagrams, etc. You can probably incorporate excerpts from these in the end product. For example if it is a training program for ferry-boat captains to convert onto a new type of vessel, you might have these kinds of specifics:

Item to be covered	Method
pre-start-up checklist	animated text sequence
electrical system	animated charts
car hoist operation	full-motion video
audio warnings	sound/diagrams
emergency doors	animated diagrams.

multimedia can be multilingual

It's very easy to design a multimedia presentation in several languages, in which case an early question on the first screen is 'What language shall we use?' followed by a menu of choices.

screen navigation

Start with clear entry points. The first screen demanding inter-activity should offer a variety of logical choices for the user to browse through and select from. These can be presented on the screen as 'buttons'. A button can be something that looks like a button, or it can be a whole text area or just a word:

Buttons:

START   HELP   DIRECTORY   QUIT

Text area:

Click anywhere in this area to see a selection of film clips

Word:
Click on any word in bold type to get more information on the item depicted. This section discusses requirements for your driver's **licence**. It shows you the kind of **cars** you might drive during training and gives you an idea of the cost.

Clicking on a word could take you to more text, a graphic or perhaps a mini video clip. This capability is called hypertext. A good multimedia program offers 'clickability' – elegant responses to mouse clicks. User-friendliness is the requirement.

multimedia checklist

■ What is the purpose of the communication, eg:
- training/education;
- reference;
- marketing;
- other?

■ Audience:
- who;
- where?

■ What are the audience's needs?

■ Delivery method (respecting audience's resources), eg:
- CD ROM, CD-I;
- online computer (type of platform);
- Internet;
- site kiosk or terminal;
- other?

■ What languages will be used?

■ What do you want the audience to do, understand, think or feel as a result of this communication?

■ What is the deadline?

■ Content outline?

■ Content media analysis?

■ What existing content can be used?

■ What new content must be created?

■ What is the budget?

■ Are there any other constraints?

■ Remarks?

writing a newsletter

A newsletter is a good way of keeping in touch with employees, clients, prospects and the media, showing that something is going on. These days, many newsletters are delivered by e-mail, which is faster, interactive and much less expensive than printed documents. Modern e-mail software enables your newsletter to have a look to it, full colour, fancy typography, pictures and hyperlinks to Web pages – in fact anything you can put on a normal Web page. Recipients need e-mail software that allows HTML (hyper-text mark-up language). If their software does not allow HTML and you send them an HTML document, they will miss all your lovely design and see the text of your newsletter surrounded by code – like this:

```
<font size=3>He said &quot;I am not an animal, I
am a <B><I>human being&#033;</I></B>&quot;<br>
```

This translates, when decoded, to:
He said 'I am not an animal, I am a *human being*!'

If you insist on a paper-based newsletter, here's where desktop publishing (DTP) comes in, because it can keep your production costs down. If you have your own DTP equipment, but you are not skilled at design, my advice is to have your newsletter professionally designed and formatted as a first step. Then your own DTP set-up can be used to create a good-looking piece by obeying the design concepts that were evolved beforehand.

A newsletter can be internal, aimed, for example, at sales or maintenance staff. The mission statement of a bimonthly newsletter for a large PR agency was: 'This is published regularly to provide our people with a useful, actionable interchange of ideas and experiences. It is intended to help you serve your clients better by bringing to your attention activities in other offices and throughout Europe, and to help you get to know our resources and people better.' Or a newsletter can be external, aimed at customers and prospects, or the journal of an association.

As such it can keep people informed of new developments, new ways of doing business, reports on activities, refinements in product lines, new customers, nifty ways of using the product, insights on regional aspects (eg, 'Who's who in the Singapore office'), special offers and so on.

If you want people to save it for reference, punch holes in it so it will fit in a binder (if it's A4, use four holes so it will fit in either a four-ring or a two-ring binder). You may want to distribute a binder with the first issue, or offer one on request, to keep costs down. Somebody ordering a binder will be a keen type!

You might want to invite the recipients of your newsletter to reproduce articles free, provided they give acknowledgement to the source. To keep tabs on this, ask them to contact you for permission to use any text or illustrations. Then you can build a file of placements that have resulted, so you know how effective the newsletter is at communicating.

A good external newsletter will help you or your client to build a relationship while offering extra opportunities to tell your story.

points about newsletters

- Simple and cheap is better than complex and expensive.
- Use a well-designed layout, with clean, easy-to-read typography and judicious use of white space.
- A second colour works wonders.
- Keep stories short, ideally no more than two pages.
- Make it lively, with lots of 'energy'.
- If possible, use pictures, charts and diagrams.
- Put a contents listing on the front cover.
- Don't overdo its frequency – gauge this to the amount of fresh news you have:
  - weekly is probably a full-time job for several people;
  - biweekly is hard work for one person;
  - monthly is okay if you can stay fresh;

- bimonthly or quarterly is probably ideal in most applications and won't overtax your resources;
- beyond quarterly is probably too infrequent unless you can hook it to some seasonal aspect.

■ Consider delivering electronically.

checklist for writing for a newsletter

■ Newsletter title?
■ Subtitle?
■ Who is the 'publisher'?
■ Frequency of issue and deadlines?
■ Audience?
■ Overall key mission (why does this newsletter exist?)
■ Other pertinent considerations/factors?
■ What is the feedback from the audience:
  - more what;
  - less what?
■ Who can contribute an article?
■ Story ideas:
  - news about the organisation;
  - financial results;
  - chairman's new-year message;
  - 'as we see it' (editorial);
  - people profiles;
  - people, office moves;
  - new developments in (department);
  - new products and services;
  - location profiles;
  - helpful hints, dos and don'ts, glossaries, guides;
  - 'how-to' stories;
  - departmental, regional, divisional 'updates';
  - reports on events, meetings, shows, exhibits, etc;
  - new business and business development;
  - customer profiles;

- new procedures;
- new advertising;
- new literature, videos, CD ROMs, etc available;
- case histories;
- war stories;
- 'what we learnt when... ';
- 'I learnt about ___ from that!';
- 'my most unforgettable day';
- 'a day in the life of... ';
- 'your questions answered';
- customer feedback and what we are doing about it;
- insights;
- users' guides;
- book reviews;
- letters column;
- new members, employees, etc;
- calendar of forthcoming events;
- what else?
■ Story prompters (see page 81):
- who?
- what?
- when?
- where?
- why?
- how?

writing for a noticeboard

Noticeboards may be physical locations or they may be computer 'bulletin boards' on an e-mail network. They carry general information that is not terribly confidential (you never know who's going to be reading them). The sort of dope that belongs on a noticeboard includes:

- holiday dates, hours and procedures;
- meeting announcements;
- 'welcome... ' (new employee announcements, with photo);
- fire drill and emergency procedures – 'floor monitors';
- announcements about new-business wins;
- internal contest results, eg sales targets;
- 'stand-up-and-be-counted' information, such as daily quality control reports, accidents on the job, etc;
- procedural information, eg use of copying machines, faxes, the new phone system, etc;
- news of community actions, charity drives, etc;
- legal requirements, eg notices of liability insurance.

computer bulletin boards

As mentioned, these can usually be accessed through the organisation's e-mail system or, if more public, through the Internet or other online service, such as AOL. If public, they tend to be affiliated with special-interest groups (SIGs), such as 'Windows users', 'Stamp collectors', 'DTP users', 'Frequent flyers', 'Americans in London' and so on.

checklist for noticeboard items

- Does this belong on the notice board?
- Which specific notice boards and where?
- Does it contain sensitive information?
- Does it have contact names and numbers?
- How else will people know of it?
- Does this update and replace something already there?
- What's the expiry date?
- Does it look good? Should it be retyped?
- Is it clear and unambiguous?

writing a press release

A press release should be about news. It should have a sense of urgency to it. If the news is time-sensitive, you may have an embargo date and time on it, eg: 'Not for release until after 2 pm Tuesday, 4 July'.

The release should be no more than two pages of double-spaced typing, with a compelling headline and introduction, accompanied perhaps by a photo. Make sure the photo has a caption, and that the press release has a contact point (names, phone and fax numbers). Your objective is to get some ink – a story, or at least a mention – in the publication. Maybe the release will prompt a call from the publication asking for more information, resulting in a story that goes into more detail.

People who get press releases get maybe 20 or more a day. So don't expect yours to be read all the way through at once. First, you have to get their attention! The headline and the opening paragraph are the most important words on the page. Then the following paragraphs, in sequence, tell the story in decreasing order of importance.

A good press release quickly answers the journalist's immediate questions (see page 81):

- ■ Who?
- ■ What?
- ■ When?
- ■ Where?
- ■ Why?
- ■ How?

Think about what kind of story the publication is looking for. Does your release deliver? It must.

Some press releases are basically for the record. They convey information about a company's activity that is not particularly newsworthy in its own right, but that a business journal such as *The Financial Times* or *The Wall Street Journal Europe* will publish as part of their mission to cover business activities within their realm of influence. Here's an example:

Jacques Phlange Joins Eurobiscuits To Head Human Resource Management

Eurobiscuits, which markets the *Biscuits du Paradis* brands, announces the appointment of Jacques Phlange to the position of Vice President, Human Resources, effective June 24, 2002, reporting directly to Helmut Schwinz, President.

Mr Phlange has 20 years of multinational human resources experience and was most recently Director, Human Resources, for EuroBrek Foods Benelux.

His responsibilities include spearheading the implementation of up-to-date professional human resource systems throughout the division and leading the development and upgrading of its overall people capability. On his appointment, Mr Phlange said: 'My mission is to stimulate an organisational climate where we recognise that to be the biscuit market leader throughout Europe, and to meet all of our other objectives, we can only achieve this through people. People are the true value of our company.'

Mr Phlange, a Frenchman, is based in Brussels. Eurobiscuits is a wholly owned subsidiary of Global Bikkies, Cincinnatti, Ohio, USA, which is itself listed on the New York Stock Exchange, symbol BIKKY, and on the national exchanges of the United Kingdom, France and Germany.

This example leaves out the essentials, such as a letterhead, contact names, dates and so on. They must be included, of course.

checklist for a press release

- ▪ Subject of press release:
  – is it really news?
- ▪ How distributed?
- ▪ Deadline for completion?
- ▪ All approvals obtained?
- ▪ Press release letterhead OK with correct names, addresses and numbers?

■ Contact names and numbers?
■ Date and time of issue?
■ Issue restrictions (eg stock market rules, etc)?
■ Is there an embargo (avoid, if possible)?
■ Audiences?
■ Should the release be tailored for different audiences:
  – international;
  – national;
  – regional;
  – local;
  – business media;
  – trade media?
■ Headline?
■ Sub-head?
■ All body text double-spaced?
■ Opening paragraph with most important part of story?
■ Why is this activity important?
■ What is the impact?
■ Who is named and quoted?
■ What are the quotes?
■ No jargon?
■ Any technicalities explained?
■ No superlatives?
■ 'Boilerplate' paragraph included:
  – standard description of issuer?
■ Ideal limit, two pages?
■ Is there a photo or other visual, with caption?

writing a business proposal

There are two types of business proposal in documentary form:
1) stand-alone document, typically submitted without any personal contact or 'walk through', eg as part of a bidding

process; 2) support document used to back up a personal presentation, which may in itself have been made on slides, overheads, computer or boards.

The distinction between the two is that the stand-alone has to carry the whole load, whereas the support is basically a reminder or reiteration of what was said by the presentation team. In fact the support presentation may be nothing more than hard copies of the slides.

stand-alone document

A stand-alone proposal will be judged in direct comparison with those submitted by your competitors – side by side. How does it stack up, not just in the quality of the ideas, the keen pricing and the obvious responsiveness to the prospect's needs, but also in look and feel?

Bear in mind that it is what is on the page that is going to determine whether you win the business or not. This means you should make the document go through a comprehensive internal vetting process after it is finished and before it is submitted. Ideally, have someone who is not close to the situation read it and make comments. Then polish it to make it as perfect as perfect can be.

support document

This is really to confirm or remind your audience of your presentation. But it is not a throw-away document. It must work just as hard as a stand-alone proposal. This is because it may need to be reviewed by people who did not attend the presentation. It may also be referred to in the evaluation process, when the prospect is figuring out to whom it will award the business. So it must be great.

contents and format

No matter how the proposal is submitted, there is a certain logic to its contents and format. Try this:

- ▓ title and subtitle;
- ▓ table of contents;
- ▓ introduction:
  - context statement;
  - who you are and how you come to be making this proposal;
- ▓ background or situation:
  - the core facts of where the prospect is right now;
- ▓ research findings (or needed) to support these facts;
- ▓ needs statement:
  - requirements suggested by the situation;
- ▓ audiences:
  - who would be impacted by the result or at whom the result is aimed;
- ▓ objectives:
  - what it is you're intending to achieve;
- ▓ strategy:
  - how you intend to achieve it;
- ▓ tactics:
  - examples of strategic solutions;
- ▓ timetable;
- ▓ budget;
- ▓ names and biographies of key players;
- ▓ other requested support documents, eg:
  - customer lists;
  - financial statement;
  - other credentials requested;
- ▓ support or background data to be put in appendices or exhibits.

style

Should you submit the proposal in prose text or bullet points, or a combination? As I've suggested, a presentation document is one of the few places where an all-bullet point style can work well. While some text in prose form makes sense, such as in the introduction, the terseness of bullet points helps a presentation document. If you do use a lot of prose, make sure you have plenty of sub-heads.

Start each new section on a new page. Allow plenty of white space and make sure the document has a structured look to it. This is easy to perform with computers and laser printers. If your organisation has a house style, so much the better, but make sure you follow it.

naming names

You must spell the client's name right! Is it SmithKline Beecham, Smith-Klein-Beecham, Smith-Kline, Beechams or what? Look at one of its business cards or an ad or a brochure or, if necessary, telephone the company and ask!

Here's a horror story I hope will never happen to you. There was the need for this proposal, scc? It turned out that the proposal document was essentially identical to one submitted to another company six months earlier, but not accepted. Thanks to the miracle of word-processing and the need for maximum efficiency, it was a simple matter to go through the computer file, do a global search and replace and change the prospect's name from the old one to the new one. That and a few new dates, and the deed was done. But the actual presentation is not the place to find out that somehow, one of the name changes didn't go through, and there is the prospect's arch rival being shown as the prospect. So if you are so lazy or efficient, or both, as to employ modern technology in this way, check every word!

checklist for proposal documents

- ■ Prospect and contact names?
- ■ Deadline for submission, where?
- ■ Deadline for completion?
- ■ How many copies are needed?
- ■ Who is in charge of the proposal at your shop?
- ■ Purpose of proposal?
- ■ Style of presentation:
  - – written, with no personal contact;
  - – personal?
- ■ Are there enclosures that must come from another source?
- ■ Are there formalities that must be complied with, eg as in a proposal to a government agency or the European Union?
- ■ Does the proposal respond precisely to the written brief, if there is one?
- ■ Does the proposal talk benefits, not features?

writing Q&A/FAQs

A question and answer sheet or FAQs (frequently asked questions) are good ways to address a complex subject. They pose the questions most likely to be asked and handle them in an easy-to-understand way.

Q **What are the benefits?**
A A Q&A helps clarify a complex topic, giving the 'official' answer to a specific question, so anyone in your organisation can respond accurately. It can also identify different angles or points of view. A good Q&A should provoke the reaction: 'Oh, that's interesting, I hadn't thought of that!' It also saves time by answering FAQs.

Q **How do we develop what questions to ask?**

A Put yourself in the place of your audience. What sorts of questions are they likely to ask? What questions would a journalist's readers ask? What questions did you ask when you first heard of the subject?

If necessary, hold a brainstorming session to identify questions. Ask your marketing, sales or customer-service staff what people want to know. Remember the old favourites: Who? What? When? Where? Why? How?

Refine and polish the wording so that both the question and the answer are absolutely clear. Read them as if you know nothing about the subject. Avoid jargon and acronyms unless explained. Don't assume the audience understands.

When you have a set of questions, establish the best sequence to put them in, eg by categories.

Q **What else is there to look out for?**

A The answers must be absolutely correct. They should be checked, double-checked and verified by the client and appropriate experts. It's a good idea to get a signature and date on the final draft to confirm this has been done.

Q **How is a Q&A distributed?**

A Usually as part of a press kit or information package, or as a dedicated page (FAQs) on a Web site.

checklist for a Q&A

■ Subject, title, etc?
■ Is it dated?
■ Is there a contact point for more information?
■ Audience?
■ How distributed?
■ Does this replace an earlier document?
■ Who needs to approve it?

writing for a sign

This may seem like a no-brainer, but it's horrifying how many confusing signs there are out there. Signs can be:

- advertising – 'Shop to let. Apply within';
- advisory – 'Trains stop at other end of platform';
- authoritarian – 'Vehicles left unattended will be towed away';
- bumper sticker braggadocio – 'We've been to Sea World';
- directional – 'Reception 2nd floor';
- informational – 'The story of the Rosetta Stone';
- locational – 'Sunken Hills Business Park';
- New York, New York – 'Don't even think of parking here!';
- polite – 'Please use the litter baskets provided';
- regulatory – 'Hard hats must be worn';
- sarcastic – 'Shoplifters will be executed';
- warning – 'Danger! 25,000 volts!'.

Consider whether the sign needs to communicate to non-English speakers, as at an airport. There are many international symbols that do that job. They are called pictograms. But, in fact, there is no globally agreed protocol for these, so you can see a sign at an airport like a suitcase, which might mean 'baggage claim', whereas at a railway station it might mean 'left luggage'.

signwriting checklist

- Purpose of sign?
- Expected life of sign?
- Location:
  - single;
  - multiple?

▓ Is it obscured by anything?
▓ Should it be unlit, lit or reflective?
▓ Does it need pictograms?
▓ Language:
   - English only;
   - what other languages?
▓ What must the sign say?
   - does it use the minimum of words;
   - is it clear and unambiguous?
▓ Is there a style it needs to conform to?

writing slides or overheads

By *slides*, I mean 35 mm colour slides projected on a screen. Slides can also be created and depicted on a computer and presented directly on a computer screen or through a projector onto a big screen. By *overheads*, I mean A4-size transparencies projected on a screen using an overhead projector.

Slides are better for large audiences, especially if you have a lot of photographic images, but the room usually needs to be darkened so that they can be seen to their best advantage. This tends to make the presentation more formal, less intimate. Overheads are great for smaller audiences and the room does not need to be darkened so much, so there is more audience involvement with the presenter. With a powerful enough projector, overheads work fine for large audiences, too. Whatever you use, hard-copy handouts can be easily made.

slides

Slides should be snappy little telegrams of what is being said. Typically, a speechmaker will not simply read the text off the slide. Often, the slide should be a picture with no words, or maybe just a chart. Which of the slides on page 116 is better?

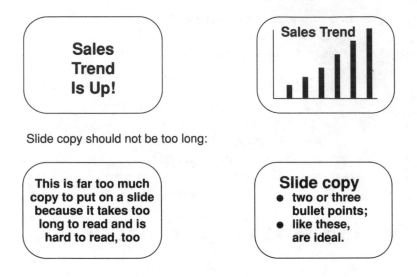

Figure 4.2 *A comparison of slide copy*

It's a good idea to storyboard a slide presentation if you have a lot of visuals. This is the same technique as used in creating a TV advertisement (see page 70). Aim to reduce the words on the slides as much as possible and let the pictures tell the story. If you are building on facts, a good technique is to present a series of slides, revealing the additional information step by step (see Figure 4.3).

But you can surely see how much better it would be to depict a series of pictures showing the actual types of vehicles causing traffic jams. You don't really need the words on the screen.

overheads

Overheads let you put more copy on the screen. They permit interactivity between the audience and presenter, who can go so far as to write on the overhead while it is being projected, so as to highlight a point or add a thought.

Slide	Speech

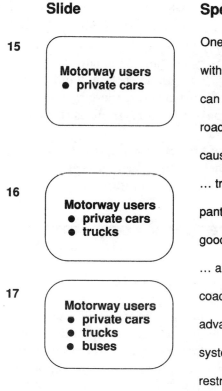

15 One of the big problems with a motorway is that it can be used by all forms of road transportation, thus causing congestion. Cars ...

16 ... trucks, lorries, trailers, pantechnicons and other goods vehicles ...

17 ... and, of course, buses and coaches can all take advantage of this transport system unless access restrictions are applied.

Figure 4.3 *Revealing the information step by step*

Production of overheads is easy if you have a laser printer. You simply print out on to transparent cells instead of paper. But be warned! The cell must be suitable for a laser or photocopier, since it needs to be heat-resistant. If you use ordinary transparencies, the first cell will melt itself on to the hot drum and run up some nasty repair costs.

Bubble-jet printers need cells especially made for them, since the transparency must accept the ink properly, because it goes onto the surface wet.

If you're into do-it-yourself, overheads are not suitable for things like colour photographs or colour charts, unless you have exotic equipment. But they are superb for quick and easy black-and-white presentations you can whip up in a few minutes on your computer. You can even use hand-drawn pictures. And there's plenty of software out there to make the job really easy. Then all you have to worry about is the actual words that go on the screen.

Once again, assume that the presenter will not actually read the words on the overhead, one-by-one. The words are there to telegraph thoughts and support the presentation.

creating slide or overhead copy from a speech

Suppose you have a speech and you need to create some slides to support it. What do you do?

Take a copy of the speech and highlight the key words in each paragraph. Aim for a new visual every 30 seconds or so.

Let's suppose you had the following speech segment, based on the Introduction to this book. The key words that could go on a slide or overhead are underlined:

> In spite of this age of the information super-highway, the World Wide Web and digital everything, never has the need for excellence in written communications been greater. Never have effective writing skills been more in demand, in business, education or government. The trend to downsizing, outsourcing, rationalisation and, these days especially, self-employment, means that people who never thought of themselves as writers must now take on that task as well as all the other responsibilities they face.

Now let's see how that might translate. Here's the storyboard, with the key words assembled, but not turned into slides yet:

	Slide	Speech
1	In spite of everything, never has the need for excellence in written communications been greater, in business, education or government.	In spite of this age of the information super-highway, the World Wide Web and digital everything, never has the need for excellence in written communications been greater. Never have effective writing skills been more in demand, in business, education or government. The trend to downsizing, outsourcing, rationalisation and, these days especially, self-employment, means that people who never thought of themselves as writers must now take on that task as well as all the other responsibilities they face.
2	People who never thought of themselves as writers must now take on that task.	

Figure 4.4 *Converting a speech into a storyboard*

Now let's turn these words into slide copy. 'In spite of everything, never has the need for excellence in written communications been greater, in business, education or government' is much too long for a slide. So we must cut this down to the essential thoughts. The same applies to 'people who never thought of themselves as writers must now take on that task'. The results are shown on page 120 (Figure 4.5).

Now, if this was a colour slide, to get some added value into it, maybe you could lay the words of slide 1 over a photograph of a computer screen showing an Internet Web page or the like. Slide 2 could show a picture of a person in a train or airline seat using a laptop computer as the background for the words.

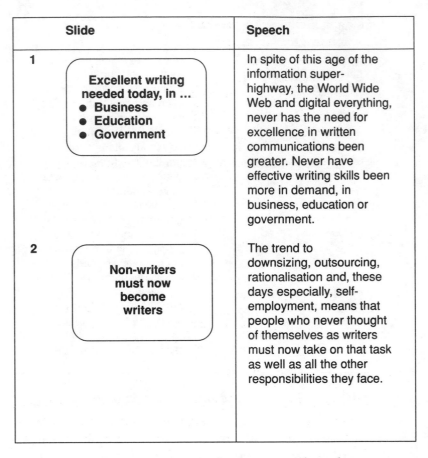

	Slide	Speech
1	**Excellent writing needed today, in ...** ● **Business** ● **Education** ● **Government**	In spite of this age of the information super-highway, the World Wide Web and digital everything, never has the need for excellence in written communications been greater. Never have effective writing skills been more in demand, in business, education or government.
2	**Non-writers must now become writers**	The trend to downsizing, outsourcing, rationalisation and, these days especially, self-employment, means that people who never thought of themselves as writers must now take on that task as well as all the other responsibilities they face.

Figure 4.5 *Converting a speech into a storyboard*

checklist for writing slides or overheads

■ Size of audience?
■ Need for interactivity?
■ Need for revision or updates in future?
■ Deadline?

▓ Which medium for presentation:
  - photographic slides;
  - computer slides;
  - overheads?
▓ In-house or outside production resource?
▓ Does the basic script exist?
▓ Are there suitable visuals that can be used?
▓ Is a hard copy handout needed?
▓ Is there a 'look' that must be followed in the design?
▓ Approval requirements?

writing a speech

Speechwriting can be fun. Or it can be horrible. Which would you prefer? This should help.

The best advice on giving a speech is 'tell 'em what you're going to tell 'em, tell 'em, then tell 'em what you told 'em'.

know your speaker

Part of the battle for the speechwriter is to know your speaker. Listen to their tone of voice and hear them saying the words as you write them. Project yourself into the room and be a part of the audience. Does it work?

The best speakers are able to hold their audiences by their sheer presence and delivery. An inspiring speaker often breaks away from the tyranny of the podium and walks around, using gesture and body language to help transmit the message. Hooray for wireless microphones. The line 'and furthermore... !' is an exciting prelude to more gems.

The deadliest speakers stand at the podium with a 50-page, closely typed script, and read it word for word in a dull, mumbly monotone. The best words they can speak are: 'finally and in conclusion, let me say... '.

preparing to write the speech

It is very important that you get a good briefing on the message, preferably from the speaker in person. Tape record this meeting so that you can capture brilliant constructions that you could never make up on your own.

Ask the speaker what the objective is. What should key members of the audience be saying as they walk out of the room after the speech? What's the 'takeaway'? What sorts of questions would the speaker like to hear from the audience? What not?

Find out how the speaker wants to work. Will they read your script word for word, or do they just want notes to guide them? Part of the issue here is the speaker's familiarity with the subject.

Does the speaker have visuals that are an essential part of the presentation? For example, charts of financial or sales performance, statements of strategy, key numbers that are pertinent. Will they be used as is, or do they need to be massaged for the presentation?

Is the speaker committed to rehearse the speech properly? This is essential for top performance.

interactive speechwriting

Some of the best moments in speechwriting are when you work with the speaker one on one in developing the script. Here's how to do it.

Start with a preliminary briefing session, maybe a day or two in advance. Get your notes from this into your computer. Then arrange a session (at least an hour, maybe two) in which you sit at the computer and the speaker sits beside you, looking at the screen. You bring the notes up onto the screen and, in conjunction with a conversation you hold with the speaker, start writing. Provided the speaker has the patience to play this game, you will end up with a beautiful speech that has the right tone of voice and says all the right things.

checklist for speechwriting

- ▓ Who is the speaker?
- ▓ Event:
  - – time of day;
  - – location?
- ▓ Deadline?
- ▓ Will it be rehearsed?
- ▓ Audience:
  - – who;
  - – how many?
- ▓ Title of speech?
- ▓ Subtitle?
- ▓ Key message?
- ▓ What's the audience 'takeaway'?
- ▓ Any visuals:
  - – existing;
  - – to be created?
- ▓ Handouts?
- ▓ Questions to encourage/anticipate?
- ▓ Questions to discourage/avoid?
- ▓ Style of script:
  - – word for word;
  - – bullet point notes?
- ▓ Autocue available or needed?
- ▓ Will speech be recorded/filmed?
- ▓ Will the media be in the audience?

writing a task description

Procter & Gamble is famous for its 'memo'. An article in *Dun's Review*, listing P&G as one of the five best-managed companies, made the following statement:

> The manager who intends to get a piece of the lucrative P&G pie first has to learn to write the P&G memo, a one-page report considered

essential to analytical thinking. The idea, of course, is that if a manager can put his or her thoughts down on paper in a concise and orderly fashion, they are, in fact, rational and orderly thoughts. Conversely, if the recommendation or analysis contains illogical elements, they are immediately apparent. Memos by the typical trainee, who writes reports and recommendations right from the start, are scrutinised with the same kind of care that a writer's story is blue-pencilled by an editor. Ruefully admits one P&G executive: 'I had to rewrite my first memo fourteen times!'

The following is based upon the 'P&G way'. The act of writing a lucid description of a task will, in itself, help clarify the points that need to be made and can often bring a fresh understanding of the problem. The discipline of laying out the key aspects in a logical order will help to identify gaps.

simplicity

Even if you are writing it just for yourself or your team, avoid jargon, and don't assume a lot of prior knowledge. If you must use jargon, explain it. The first time you use an acronym, explain it. Never assume, or you will make an *ass* out of *u* and *me*.

audiences

Before you start, you must have an absolutely clear idea of who the readers will be. Always write with the most uninformed member of your audience in mind.

format

Here's a basic format to follow when creating such a document. You don't have to be rigid about it:

■ purpose of document;

- ▓ an overview of the problem and the solution proposed or needed in no more than one or two paragraphs;
- ▓ situation:
  - the core facts of where we are right now;
- ▓ background:
  - relevant information supporting the situation, eg:
    - competitive, legislative, economic, historic problems;
- ▓ considerations:
  - aspects that must be considered in evolving a solution:
    - timing;
    - finance;
    - capabilities;
  - available or needed resources;
- ▓ audiences:
  - who are impacted by the result or at whom the result is aimed;
- ▓ objectives:
  - what it is you're intending to achieve;
- ▓ strategy:
  - by what means you intend to achieve it;
- ▓ tactics:
  - examples of solutions;
- ▓ discussion (optional):
  - a brief review of the pros and cons of different courses of action;
  - rejected approaches and why they were dropped.

writing a video script

Involve a production company or facility from the beginning. Start the process with a briefing session in which the communications objective, audiences and messages are all made clear.

What is the tape for? How will it be distributed? Is it to be shown on a 16-screen videowall at the World Travel Market at Olympia, or is it to be sent out to people wanting more information? Will it be shown by the sales people to prospects when on a sales call? Will it run, unattended, in the lobby of the client's building? What are the deadlines? This kind of briefing is given to a production company, and you might invite competitive bids.

To write the script, start with a treatment, which is a few pages outlining the creative approach you propose. Think about the visuals. Are you going to shoot original material or use existing footage? Always, always, think about the audience. What do you want them to get from the video?

Some productions can be made using existing footage, perhaps artfully combined with new material. If you have made a video news release, or vox pops ('person-in-the-street' interviews), these could very easily find their way into your production if that style would work.

Avoid sequences in which non-professionals have to deliver lines. Real people should speak in their own voices and talk extemporaneously. If you must have them deliver specific lines, consider doing them voice-over relevant visuals, rather than having them on camera stiltedly delivering someone else's words. If necessary, use an autocue (teleprompter), which delivers the lines to wherever the person is looking.

shooting script

Figure 4.6 is an example of the format for a shooting script.

checklist for a video script

■ Title?
■ Subtitle?
■ Purpose/use of programme?
■ Communications objective?

Video	Audio
camera instructions and activities go here	sound, words and music go here
1. OPEN ON SHOT OF CAMERA CREW SHOOTING ON A SET	MUSIC: Stock
SUPER TITLE HOW TO MAKE A VIDEO	MUSIC FADES UNDER...
2. DISSOLVE TO PRESENTER STANDING BY CAMERA WITH VIDEOWALL IN BG	PRESENTER (to camera) Producing your own video can be quite a challenge.
3. CUT TO MONTAGE OF SCENES FROM VIDEOS ON VIDEOWALL	PRESENTER (VO) Hundreds of corporate videos are produced every year. With today's emphasis on keeping costs down, many companies have decided to do it themselves.
etc, etc	etc, etc

Figure 4.6   *Sample of a shooting script format*

- ▓ Audiences?
- ▓ Messages?
- ▓ What's the audience 'takeaway'?
- ▓ Working budget?
- ▓ Production company/facility?
- ▓ Deadlines?
- ▓ Approval process?

- ■ How will it be distributed?
- ■ Treatment?
- ■ Creative approach?
- ■ Who are the players?
- ■ Shooting locations?
- ■ Original material?
- ■ Existing footage?
- ■ Visuals/graphics:
  - – existing;
  - – to be created?
- ■ Music?

writing a Web site

It is worthwhile employing the services of a competent Web site designer if you're new to Web sitery. A DIY site generally looks that way. But avoid excessive irrelevant animation, which many designers love. Most people won't have the patience to wait while a complex page loads. Good advice is to note one or two sites you like, then find out and contact whoever did them. Navigation on your site should be so easy that no one is more than three quick clicks away from finding what they want.

Keep the writing tight. Don't lay out great wide areas of text that require back-and-forth horizontal scrolling to read every line. People tend to *look at* rather than *read* text on Web sites. Use a few small images, headings and bullet point text rather than long paragraphs. Keep it simple so loading times are short.

Web site checklist

- ■ What is the purpose of the Web site, eg:
  - – corporate information;
  - – obtaining feedback?

▨ Product/service information?
▨ Customer support?
▨ Sales of goods off the page?
▨ Press releases?
▨ Recruiting:
  – what else?
▨ Audience:
  – who
  – where?
▨ What are the audience's needs?
▨ What languages will be used?
▨ What do you want the audience to do, understand, think or feel as a result of visiting this Web site?
▨ What absolutely *must* be on the site?
▨ What is the deadline?
▨ Content outline?
▨ What existing content can be used?
▨ What new content must be created?
▨ What is the budget?
▨ Are there any other constraints?
▨ How will the site be kept up to date?
▨ Remarks?

writing a CV/resumé

The number of people seeking any given nationally advertised job can literally be in the thousands. So how are you going to make sure your application is put on the correct pile?

the covering letter and CV

Bear in mind you have about 10 seconds to make your first impression. Your covering letter should be no more than three paragraphs, plus some bullet point highlights. Your CV should fit on one page. Everything should be immaculate, with no spelling mistakes. Certainly no erasures or white-outs. Ideally, have your letter and CV word-processed and laser printed. There are plenty of organisations that can do this for you, such as Prontaprint or Kall-Kwik on most high streets. There are also companies that specialise in creating CVs for you (you'll see them advertised near the appointments section of the major newspapers). Take a look at *Preparing Your Own CV*, by Rebecca Corfield, published by Kogan Page.

On the next two pages are examples of an effective covering letter and CV. In the letter, notice that it should echo key points in the advertisement. The CV is written in reverse chronological order, with the most recent events first and so on. Under each job we have the title and a brief, bullet-point précis of the tasks or major accomplishments. Salary details should be excluded in the first instance. If they ask you to give your present salary in the initial contact, put it in the letter and indicate other perks, such as a car (give the type of car as well, eg, BMW 320i) and key benefits.

There is no law against age discrimination in employment in the United Kingdom (it is illegal in the United States and many other enlightened countries), so it is not uncommon to see an age range specified in a job advertisement. If you fall outside of the age range, but are otherwise qualified, omit your age, or you will simply be rejected out of hand.

If you have other relevant skills, such as languages, include these.

covering letter

Dear Mr Smith:

I read with interest your advertisement in *The Sunday Times*, 30 June 2002, for Senior Account Managers. I would like to be considered for one of these positions and I have enclosed a brief CV for your review.

I believe that I have all of the attributes demanded for a position of this calibre, for example:

- ▮ the ability to take a complex and intangible 'product' and communicate the benefits simply and concisely;
- ▮ the ability to maintain outstanding client relationships, and a belief in partnership selling;
- ▮ a track record of success in sales and marketing to major European and UK corporations, with primary contact at Finance Director or Treasury level;
- ▮ an entrepreneurial approach towards securing new business.

Although much of my sales and marketing experience comes from the financial services industry, I was highly successful in the IT sector while at ABCDE Computer Systems, Plc.

I look forward to hearing from you.

Yours sincerely

Your Name Here
Senior Sales Executive

EXPERIENCE

- Business Development Manager, **XYZ Asset & Project Finance**, Redhill, 1998–present
  - Develop university finance projects
  - £25 m mandated business in nine months
  - Develop private sector finance for Housing Association projects
- Marketing Manager, **MNOPQ Leasing & Finance Co**, London, 1996–1998
  - Big-ticket asset-based finance
  - New business development
- Sales Executive, **ABCDE Computer Systems PLC**, Reading, 1992–1996
  - Mainframe computer-lease packaging
  - 100 per cent club, exceeded one-year sales target in eight months
- Principal, **NameBrand Properties**, Crawley 1988–1992
  - Property selection, financing, acquisition, renovation, management
  - Financing and leasing negotiations
  - Town planning department negotiations
  - Historic commercial/residential properties
  - Own business, record of success and profit

EDUCATION

- Welgar College, Northampton – Bachelor of Arts, Psychology

PERSONAL

- Married, two children 14 & 9, excellent health

ADDRESS & TELEPHONE

the need to communicate ideas

The best way to teach someone to drive is to put them in a car and have them handle the controls, after a demonstration and with verbal and operative guidance from an instructor. The best way to understand a foreign country is to go there and experience it: ride in their trains, eat in their restaurants, work with their people, shop in their shops, watch their television.

Yet our task, as writers, is to enable our readers to replace the world of actual experience with the world of description. We have to cause them to undergo a simulation of the desired experience with our carefully chosen and crafted words.

This chapter is about presenting ideas meaningfully. See also page 43, on the use of visuals.

present well-reasoned arguments

Very often when you are writing a document you need to show your thinking in arriving at a conclusion or recommendation. You have examined the files, reports and records that bear upon the problem. You've reviewed the market research data. You've drawn upon the knowledge and experience of your colleagues. Now it is time to make a point.

Using your own know-how, background and judgement, consider the various methods of reasoning to determine which method or combination is best suited to your task. Four good ways of doing this are:

- ■ inductive reasoning;
- ■ deductive reasoning;
- ■ cause-and-effect relationships;
- ■ analogies.

inductive reasoning

This involves the examination of typical instances or examples, so as to reach a general conclusion. It moves from the specific to the general. However, it needs to be based on a sufficient number of examples or instances to warrant the conclusion, and these instances must be typical and pertinent to the problem.

For example: 'Harry left his car unlocked and his camera was stolen off the front seat. Jane left her car unlocked and her handbag was stolen off the front seat. If I leave my car unlocked with something of value on the seat, it will probably be stolen.'

deductive reasoning

This applies a general principle, background of knowledge or rule to a specific example. It moves from the general to the specific, or from a conclusion to a specific support. Again, you need enough examples for the conclusion to be realistic.

For example: 'London has a high rate of street crime, as does any large city. I will not leave my car unlocked when parking on the street.'

cause-and-effect relationships

This method, simply, involves searching for the effect when you know the cause, or vice versa. Check to see whether the cause is sufficient to produce the effect, and whether there are other causes that could produce the same effect. Also, establish the link between cause and effect directly and logically.

For example: 'If interest rates go up, the housing market will suffer, because costs will rise.'

analogies

This method takes one instance or event and, by comparing it with another instance or event, attempts to conclude that what happened in one instance will happen in another.

For example: 'Direct rather than brokered car insurance has sold well. Direct rather than brokered household insurance should sell well.'

use examples

Examples help clarify the points you are making. Use them as often as possible, as I have in this book. The more realistic you can make them, the more powerful they will be. Consider this:

Bloggs and Co, based in Anytown, wanted to introduce a new widget. They called in three advertising agencies, gave them each a brief and invited proposals. The agencies went away and worked on the problem, then came back and presented their ideas. The one that seemed to have the best solution won the contract.

Compare that with this:

When Federal Express started advertising its overnight package-delivery service in 1974, it had the good fortune to select New York-based Ally

& Gargano as its advertising agency. A&G's brilliant TV commercials, involving humour and real-life situations, were a major reason that Federal Express took off so fast.

Perhaps the most memorable of these featured fast-talking Joe Moschitta covering 130 words in 30 seconds in a spot called 'Fast-Paced World'. If you've seen it, you'll remember it. The last few moments featured moustachioed Moschitta, in the role of a time-conscious CEO, on the phone saying: 'Dick-what's-the-deal-with-the-deal? Are-we-dealing? Dave-it's-a-deal-with-Don-Dork-and-Dick. Dick-it's-a-Dork-with-Don-deal-and-Dave. Dave-gotta-go, disconnecting. Dick-gotta-go, disconnecting... ' while the voice-over announcer wraps it up with 'Federal Express. When it absolutely, positively has to be there overnight.'

I think you'll agree that the second example was more interesting than the first. That's because it was real, not phony.

Use examples to illustrate your point, to make things absolutely clear. Examples can come from your own experience and that of colleagues, from the media, especially the trade press of your industry, and from customers and other people on the front lines of your business. When you're citing an example, use language that will help your reader visualise what you are saying (as in the FedEx example, above).

the need to get on with it

This chapter is about producing. Getting it done. It assumes that by now you know what it is you have to do. So how do you do it?

plan your work

In order to plan your work you need to know several things so as to allocate time and resources realistically:

- the deadline;
- the delivery;
- the task;
- the size of the task;
- the need for research;
- the need for interviews;
- the contributing resources;
- the approval/acceptance process;
- other work you have in progress;
- unavoidable interruptions, eg Christmas;

- ▓ timetable;
- ▓ budget.

the deadline

'Deadlines are *sacred*', says Mike Johnson, author of the helpful book *Business Buzzwords*, and a former magazine editor. When you commit to a deadline you *must* keep it. The penalty for missing a deadline is *death*. Commitment means doing something with the same amount of enthusiasm as you displayed when you said you would do it.

So when you agree a deadline, be realistic, taking into account all of the items mentioned in the list above. Excuses like: 'I'll try to get it done for you as soon as I can, hopefully,' are *unacceptable*. See page 142 for how to build a timetable.

the delivery

What constitutes delivery of the finished work? Printed magazines in the newsagents? A fax of the final draft? An e-mail of the text? A computer disk of the file? Mailed hard copy to the head office? How many copies are needed? Does it need to be processed between you and the client (eg printed, copied, bound, etc)?

the task

What do you have to do? An article on something you know nothing about? An article on something you know *everything* about? A pamphlet? A book? A speech? A script? What is it?

the size of the task

Before you start, you need an idea of the volume of writing you have to end up with. Is it a 1,000-word article? A 12-page newsletter? A 6-panel pamphlet? A 20-minute speech? A 10-minute video script? A 30-second radio commercial? It is helpful to be aware of how fast you write. Can you churn out 10,000 words a day or do you flounder around trying to come up with 500? Take a look at what you have done lately and get in mind a personal writing rate. Obviously the more you know about a subject, the faster you can write about it. Which brings us to...

the need for research

How much research will you have to do? Will you receive any support, or must you do it all yourself? There are people called researchers, and that's all they do. You'll find them listed in *The Writer's Handbook* under 'Editorial, Research and Other Services'.

Sometimes you are given a whole load of material for reference, which inevitably consists of 80 pages of tenth generation photocopies (partly unreadable) and 24 pages of refaxed assemblies of various four- and five-page faxes from different sources with no logical overall page numbering system (12 pages of which are also in the unreadable photocopies, it turns out).

the need for interviews

Very often you'll find you need to interview some people to get input on the story. This may be for background information or to get quotes.

How you do the interview has a big bearing on time management. Do you have to go to several people's offices and sit down with them for half an hour or more? Can you handle it by phone? This is obviously preferable from a time point of view. See page 147 for more on interviewing.

the contributing resources

It might be that a section of the piece is to come from some-body else – an expert or specialist, for example. This may need to be rewritten, or certainly edited to make it work with the other contents. The key problem here is that the contributor may not understand the meaning of deadlines (see above). The weakest excuses for non-delivery will be heard (flat tyre? flu? they need input themselves from someone who is on holiday?).

If you have the vaguest suspicion that the contributor will fail to deliver on time, take all possible measures to overcome this. For example, a few days before their deadline, have a conversation designed to assure yourself that all is well and on schedule. If you spot danger signals, you have been warned!

Ideally, get the contributor to give you a disk of their text, or send it to you by e-mail, to avoid the need to reinput it. Alternatively, if you have a scanner with OCR (optical char-acter recognition) software, you can probably read the printed text right into your machine.

The biggest problems occur when one of you is using archaic technology, or no technology at all, and the other is using the latest software. You can waste a lot of time trying to overcome this. Work it out in advance. Don't assume the disk they send you will work in your machine. Specify the system (eg Macintosh OS 9.1, Windows 98, etc) and the software (eg Microsoft Word, Apple Works, etc). Usually Macs will read both Windows and Mac files, while PCs using Windows will only read Windows.

the approval/acceptance process

You must build time into your schedule for approvals if they are needed. It may be that different people must approve different sections of the piece.

The time you allow must include the time taken to deliver and return the copy, the time for them to read it and the time to fix it if there's a problem (and then possibly go through the whole approval process *again*!).

other work in process

Rarely will you have to write something as your only task. Usually you have other projects underway. Their time and resource consumption must be considered, too. You may have to reprioritise your work to get it all done efficiently.

unavoidable interruptions, eg Christmas

How dare people take time off for holidays, sick leave, religious festivals, etc! Don't they understand the importance of your project? When you're working out your timetable (see below), use a good calendar to identify and respect the inevitable impositions by the outside world. Humbug!

checklist for planning your work

- ▓ Title of project?
- ▓ Task?
- ▓ Deadline?
- ▓ Delivery:
  - form;
  - location?
- ▓ Size of task?
- ▓ Research:
  - available;
  - to be carried out?
- ▓ Interviews:
  - who;
  - where?

- ■ Translations?
- ■ Design, layout, typography?
- ■ Illustrations, photography?
- ■ Contributing resources?
- ■ Approval/acceptance process?
- ■ Other work you have in progress?
- ■ Unavoidable interruptions?
- ■ Timetable?
- ■ Budget?

work out a timetable

The more complex the job, the more you need a timetable. This should show the steps, the deadlines or milestones for each step and show who is responsible for completing each one. The timetable then becomes the key tool in managing the project. It will help you watch your deadlines and take corrective action if you see a problem coming to the surface.

Here's a typical simple timetable, for an industry year-book, containing advertising. It is composed of some original material and a lot of copy submitted by members of the trade association. Joe is the client, Tina is the editor, Fred is in charge of advertising sales, AD is the Art Director and Harry is in charge of production:

Item	Start	End	Who?
Approval to proceed	11 Dec	18 Dec	Joe
Evolution of contents plan	18 Dec	22 Jan	Tina
Agreement to contents plan	22 Jan	29 Jan	Joe/Tina
Appoint art director (AD)	22 Jan	29 Jan	Joe/Tina
Advertising rate card available	22 Jan	5 Feb	Fred
Preliminary layout concepts	29 Jan	5 Feb	AD
Completion of content copy	29 Jan	29 Apr	Tina
Advertising sales	5 Feb	24 Jun	Fred
Editing, revisions completed	29 Apr	27 May	Tina

Layout dummy completed	27 May	8 Jun	AD
Agreement to whole book	8 Jun	24 Jun	Joe/Tina
Production and printing	24 Jun	2 Sep	Harry
Delivery	2 Sep	16 Sep	Harry

the process

Here's how to work out a timetable:

1. Identify the steps that need to be taken.
2. Put the steps in chronological order.
3. Calculate or guesstimate the amount of time each step will take to complete, in days or weeks.
4. Start at the delivery date and work backwards.
5. Work out start and end dates for each step.
6. Assemble the timetable in chronological order by end date.

identify steps and sequence

Here's a list of typical action steps of a printed document, such as a brochure, in their approximate chronological order:

▓ assignment of project, budget, approval to proceed;
▓ research and information gathering;
▓ outline;
▓ approval of outline;
▓ briefing of other resources:
  - copy contributions;
  - design;
  - visuals:
    - photography;
    - illustrations;
    - graphics/charts;
  - printer;

- creation of first draft;
- approvals to first draft;
- rewrites/editing;
- final draft;
- layout concepts;
- approvals;
- production, typography, layout;
- printing;
- delivery.

calculate time for each step

Develop your own guidelines for each assignment. How long will it take to do five interviews over the phone? How long will it take to do five interviews if you have to fly to Zurich and meet each person individually in their office? How long will it take to go to the library and research the literature? How long will it take to access the database and get all the figures you need? How long will it take to manipulate the figures and make charts? How long will it take you to write 10,000 words of copy? How long will Serena take to write 10,000 words of copy? How long will 'Legal' take to approve the first draft? How long will it take to amend the first draft after the initial approval process? And so on.

You'll have to make a judgement, based on the amount of work involved and your own experience. Work in days or weeks, and allow a little leeway to compensate for unexpected events (remember Murphy's Law: if something can go wrong, it will go wrong and at the worst possible time).

work backwards from delivery date

Get a calendar and look at the delivery date. Where do you have to deliver and in what form? What day of the week is it? Think of weekends and national holidays. In space shuttle countdown terms, the delivery date is 'T'. Everything before that is 'T minus...'. So if you have to print 10,000 copies of the brochure and deliver them to the trade fair in Frankfurt by noon Monday 23 September 2002, they need to be shipped from the printer in Luton by when? Let's say they need to be out of the door in Luton and into the courier's hands no later than Friday 20 September at 1600. That's T minus three days.

If the printer says it will take one week to print, that means you have to have the materials to Luton by Friday 13 September. What are the materials? Camera-ready copy, film or computer disk? T minus 10 days.

If the production people say it will take a week to prepare the materials for printing, that means you have to have the copy, disks and artwork to the production people by Friday 6 September. But you will want to see a proof and have the opportunity to make corrections. Let's say this takes three days. So back up three days from 6 September to Tuesday 3 September. T minus 20 days.

But the copy you send to the production people must be approved, so you need to allow, let's say, one week for this, including time to make corrections. So you have to get the final draft to the approver by Tuesday August 27. But guess where she will be on that day? On her summer holidays, natch! So find out where she's going to be and fax it to her there! Silly little things like vacations cannot get in the way of commerce! Obviously you'll need to work this out in advance of her trip. We're at T minus 27 days.

Of course, you will have had to write the copy and assemble the contributions coming from outside sources. And you'll have had to interface with the designer to make sure the brochure is coming together properly. Three weeks? Plus a few days. Say 3 August is your start date. That's T minus 51 days.

You'll need to have conducted some research and interviews to get the project going. Say one week. Start 27 July. T minus 58 days.

And, you need a go ahead and budget approval. Say you got that on 25 July. That's T minus 60 days. And that's how you do it. Here's the resultant timetable:

Item	Start	End	Who?
Approval to proceed	25 Jul	25 Jul	Jane
Research and interviews	27 Jul	3 Aug	Tina
Write copy/do design ideas	3 Aug	27 Aug	Tina/AD
Approvals	27 Aug	3 Sep	Jane
Copy to production	3 Sep	10 Sep	Tina/AD
Approval of proof	10 Sep	13 Sep	Tina/AD
Production and printing	13 Sep	20 Sep	Harry
Delivery in Frankfurt	20 Sep	23 Sep	Harry

The most important thing in preparing a timetable is to make allowances for the correct sequence of events, in conformity with each other. You may need the photos of the new car for the brochure by 15 June. But the car will not be available to photograph until 22 June. What does that do to your schedule? Trade fair opening dates are rigid. Other events are more flexible. So you must allow for everything that could happen to get in the way and still not screw up your project.

how to budget

Budgeting a job is an important part of the task of business writing. You need to have a clear idea of what a project will cost before you start. If things look like they'll change enough during the process to affect the budget you need to know about this as early as possible to determine what to do about it.

You can construct a budget once you have an idea of the various costs. The items that would go into a printed document budget, and how they are typically charged, are these:

- research (daily rate or rate for the job);
- copy/scriptwriter (rate per 1,000 words or rate for the job);
- photography (daily rate or rate for the job);
- other illustrations/graphics (rate for the job);
- translations (rate per 1,000 words);
- design (rate for the job);
- typesetting (rate per 1,000 words or rate for the job);
- printing (rate based on specifications and quantities);
- deliveries, copies, faxes, travel, etc (at cost).

You may also have internal management fees or departmental overhead charges to apply. For budgeting information on items such as video, radio, multimedia and so on, talk to a specialist in the field.

typical budget

Here's how a budget for a brochure might look:

research	£500
copywriting	£2,500
photography	£1,800
design and typesetting	£2,500
printing	£6,000
deliveries, copies, faxes, etc	£200
total budget (plus VAT, if applicable)	£13,500

how to interview

When you are preparing a document it is vitally important that you talk to those in the know. They are the most informed people on the subject and give you insights that won't come up in a written brief or someone else's interpretation of the facts.

interviewing methods

The best way to interview is in person, sitting face to face. Second best is over the telephone. Third choice is to supply written questions and wait for written answers. This last method can work extremely well if the interviewee is literate and expresses words well. It can be a horror story otherwise and may require several clarifications and further questions.

taping

Ideally you should tape record a personal or telephone interview. Ask if it's all right to do this. Refusals are rare, although it's not unusual for the person to ask you to stop recording if they get into a sensitive area. If you're doing a lot of taping, for example a series of several people, one after the other, start each new person on a new cassette. Make sure the cassettes are clearly labelled. If your budget can stand it, get the tapes professionally transcribed and have the transcriber give you the transcription on disk so that you can work it into your piece more efficiently. You can get transcriptions done overnight in the major centres. Look in the *Yellow Pages* under 'Secretarial Services'.

quotes

Quotes bring a story to life, so seek them out. If you hear a wonderful line, say 'May I quote you on that?' and then make sure you capture the words accurately. There's nothing wrong with saying 'I need a quote from you, what can you say about this?' You can even write a quote and say 'Are you comfortable with this as a quote from you?'

probing

Probing allows you to seek and obtain the information you need during an interview. There are two types of probes: open and closed.

open probes

These are questions that generally take more than a few words to answer and hence are very useful in the interviewing process. You want to encourage interviewees to talk, to express freely what is on their minds.

Open probes help direct questions to topics of importance, eliciting the views, perceptions, knowledge and concerns of the person. They help you get plenty of useful information, fast. Here are some examples of open probes:

- 'Tell me about this programme.'
- 'Can you give me a couple of examples of this?'
- 'How was this received by the public?'
- 'Why is this important to you?'

closed probes

These are questions that can usually be answered in one or two words ('yes', 'no', '19', etc). Use them to help verify or quantify an item of information. Since they let you direct the conversation to a topic of your own choosing, they can be most useful when you need to verify your grasp of something the person has said.

They are also helpful to get a person who seems unwilling to talk freely to open up, or when you need specific information to complete your understanding of the situation. Here are some examples of closed probes:

- 'How long have you been in this business?'
- 'Is it true that... ?'
- 'Which of these examples is correct?'
- 'If I understand you properly, you're saying... Is that so?'

listening

Why do we have so much difficulty in listening to people? Is it because they are basically boring and have little of any interest to tell us (because we know what we are going to hear)? Because we are seeking confirmation, not information? Because what's being said is getting in the way of what needs to be said? Well they could certainly be some of the barriers to listening. Listening is in fact something we have to perform actively to become good writers.

The advantages of listening are that your attention will be more focused on the matter at hand and you will get more information. If you listen, you can proceed with the task.

The late Geoff Nightingale, president of SynerGenics, gave these rules of listening:

■ Listen for ideas, not facts – ask yourself what they mean.
■ Judge content, not delivery, ie *what* they say, not how they say it.
■ Listen optimistically – don't lose interest straight away.
■ Don't jump to conclusions.
■ Adjust your note-taking to the speaker, ie, be flexible.
■ Concentrate – don't start dreaming – and keep eye contact.
■ Do not think ahead of the speaker – you'll lose track.
■ Work at listening – be alert and alive.
■ Keep emotions under control when listening.
■ Open your mind – practise accepting new information.
■ Breathe slowly and deeply.
■ Relax physically, get comfortable.

Active listening involves playing back your own interpretation of what has been said in acknowledgement – 'I see. Let me see if I understand you. As I get it, what you mean is...'.

making notes

Even if you tape record an interview, it still makes sense to make notes. Assuming you don't take shorthand, what's the best way of doing this? You can use two techniques. One is just to assemble the information as it comes, using headings and a series of bullet points, not unlike the way this book is structured. Always leave plenty of room to add in more information under a heading later.

The second way is 'mind mapping'. Below, you'll find an example of how a mind map might start on the subject of this book. Each chapter is assigned a 'branch'. Then from these branches you would hang the sub-sections. From each of these you would hang the key thoughts. Obviously you need a fairly large piece of paper for mind mapping.

The advantage of mind mapping is that it records the information more digitally than a set of hierarchical notes, so you can add further thoughts in the right place as they occur.

Figure 6.1 *Example of the beginning of a mind map*

how to get started when you are at a loss for words

In the olden days, there were things called typewriters and pens. They used a substance called paper to receive the symbols known as writing that were applied by the writer.

The biggest problem the writer had was a blank piece of paper. Ernest Hemingway called it 'The White Bull'. You wanted to write something and there was this rectangular white sheet sitting there taunting you. So you wrote something and it was not good, which brought you to the best thing about writing onto a sheet of paper, which is that it crumples up into a ball very well so that you could throw it into the wastebasket if you didn't like what you had written but were otherwise having a good day, or miss it completely if you were not.

Now we have computers and screens. The screen can be made to have anything on it. It doesn't crumple up very well, but you can consign something to computer limbo with a satisfying sense of dispatch by pushing the right combination of keys.

If you're having trouble getting started with some writing, write anything. Write the words from the brief, or the title. Make up something outrageous about the subject and write that. I never throw any computer file away, so I've got just about everything I've written in the last 10 years on some disk or other. When I have to write something new and I can't get started, I'll find a file of a similar item, put that on the screen and start rewriting that into the new subject matter. The secret of being able to write is to start writing.

use the writer's aids

The essential tools for any writer are:

- a dictionary;
- a thesaurus;
- a style book;
- computer spelling/grammar checker;
- a book of quotations;
- writers' reference books;
- writers' Web sites;
- libraries.

dictionaries help you get going

Since a good way to start writing a document is to define your terms of reference precisely, a dictionary can be immensely helpful to the creative process as well as providing a source of accuracy.

thesaurus

Dr Peter Mark Roget took his first shot at what he called 'a system of verbal classification... a classed catalogue of words' in 1805. In the preface to the first edition of his *Thesaurus*, published in 1852, he referred to his earlier work:

I had often found this little collection, scanty and imperfect as it was, of much use to me in literary composition, and had often contemplated its extension and improvement; but a sense of the magnitude of the task, amidst a multitude of other avocations, deterred me from the attempt. Since my retirement from the duties of Secretary of the Royal Society, I resolved to embark on an undertaking which, for the last three or four years, has given me incessant occupation, and has, indeed, imposed upon me an amount of labour very much greater than I had anticipated...

Nicely, if quaintly, intricately, elaborately, complicatedly put, Dr Roget. Those words, as read today, might be called unnecessarily pedantic, somewhat punctilious, scrupulous and meticulous if not fastidious, nay even Victorian. But thank you, Dr Roget. The thesaurus is a constant and valued aid to we writers. I have one on my Macintosh, called Word Finder. If you're looking for ideas, you click on the word in question, press a couple of keys and get a result, consequence, development, end, fruit, harvest, issue, outcome, payoff, product, progression, ramification, reward...

style book

There are various style books available. Using one will help you write right. The most obvious are Fowler's *Modern English Usage* and Gowers' *Complete Plain Words*. The Plain Language Commission's founder Martin Cutts has written *The Plain English Guide*. And then there's *A Good Guide to English in the 21st Century*, by Godfrey Howard.

Some style books are published by organisations to show their preferred approach to writing, punctuation, spelling and presentation. Examples are *The Economist Style Guide* and *Waterhouse on Newspaper Style*, which was written for the Daily Mirror. For a US approach, try *The Elements of Style* by Strunk and White.

You can also get software such as *The Oxford Writer's Shelf*, which contains *The Oxford Mini Dictionary*, *The Guide to English Usage*, *The Mini Dictionary of Quotations* and *The Dictionary for Writers and Editors*. Not bad for £65.

If you are writing for a specific publication or publisher, ask if they have their own style guide. Kogan Page has its eight-page *Notes for Authors*, for example. Here's an excerpt:

1. Jargon
Jargon should be kept to an absolute minimum. Where it is unavoidable it should, on first usage, be clearly explained for the benefit of the reader.

2. Spelling
Where there are alternative ways of spelling the same word, please be consistent. This applies particularly to words that are sometimes hyphenated, eg cooperation/co-operation. Please also try to keep the spelling of words that can take 'z' or 's', eg, realise, organise, consistent throughout.
3. Capitalisation
Please be consistent. Please keep capitals to a minimum. Do not use capital letters for words like manager, company, etc. Use *italic*, **bold** or underlining rather than capitals for emphasis.
4. Full stops
Full stops can be kept to a minimum and should not be used in postal codes or in the initials of well-known organisations such as NATO, UNESCO, BBC, IPD etc. They are also unnecessary in eg, ie, etc, col, p, pp and so on.
5. Acronyms and abbreviations
Acronyms should be spelt out the first time they are used, eg, Institute of Chartered Accountants in England and Wales (ICAEW). Thereafter, the acronym only should be used. Do not use abbreviations unless you want the words to appear in abbreviated form in the text, eg, hrs, mins, vol. If your manuscript, owing to the nature of the subject matter, involves the use of large numbers of acronyms it would help ease of reference for the reader if you supplied a glossary of meanings.

use a computer spelling/grammar checker

Most sophisticated computer word-processing software has a built-in spelling checker. This often comes in either UK or US spelling, so make sure you're using the right kind. You can add your own custom dictionary of words, such as proper names, brand names, or common acronyms. The beauty of the spelling checker is that it will not only catch wrongly spelt words, but also silly transcription typos, such as teh for the or olny for only. However, it will not catch the incorrect uses of homonyms, such as there instead of their or where instead of were. For that you need a grammar checker.

A grammar checker is a separate utility that you can run parallel to your word-processing program. It will check not only grammar, but usage, punctuation and style as well as spelling. It will watch out for things like double negatives, improper pronouns and prepositions, and will check for overly long sentences. It can be customised to your own writing style. Some software will even analyse the writing according to readability indexes, such as Gunning Fog.

quotations

> The two most engaging powers of an author are to make new things familiar, familiar things new.
>
> William Makepeace Thackeray

Yes. A nifty quotation can work wonders in helping you tell your story. You can always find one that will suit:

■ Editing?

Not that the story need be long, but it will take a long while to make it short

Henry David Thoreau

■ Ideas?

Everything has been thought of before, but the problem is to think of it again

Johann W von Goethe

■ Speeches?

If you cannot say what you have to say in 20 minutes, you should go away and write a book about it

Lord Brabazon

■ Accuracy?

A falsehood once received from a famed writer becomes traditional to posterity

John Dryden

■ Writing?

I love being a writer. What I can't stand is the paperwork

Peter de Vries

■ Royalties?

Sir, no man but a blockhead ever wrote except for money

Samuel Johnson

■ Criticism?

Your manuscript is both good and original; but the part that is good is not original, and the part that is original is not good

Samuel Johnson

A good book of quotations belongs on your shelf.

writer's reference books

The Writer's Handbook, by Barry Turner, is published each year and contains a vast array of really useful material. It is particularly valuable if you freelance or seek to make money from your writing. Then there's *The Writers' and Artists' Yearbook*. Another helpful work is the *Blackwell Guide for Authors*, which discusses many of the intricacies of authorship, particularly in the area of dealing with publishers.

writers' Web sites

As you might expect, there are thousands of resources to help writers on the Web. That all-powerful search engine, Google, has an excellent directory of these, which lists everything a writer might need, under these headings:

■ agents;
■ book writing;
■ children's writing;
■ collaboration;
■ conferences;
■ contests;
■ copy editing;
■ creative writing;
■ directories;
■ editing services;
■ fiction;

- freelancing;
- individual writers and resumés;
- journaling;
- markets;
- non-fiction;
- organisations;
- personal pages;
- playwriting;
- poetry;
- publications;
- publishers;
- research;
- screenwriting;
- self-publishing;
- software;
- songwriting;
- style guides;
- Web rings;
- workshops and courses;
- writers chat;
- writing services;
- writing tips;
- young writers.

You'll find it on:
http://directory.google.com/Top/Arts/Writers_Resources/

libraries

Robert McKee, in his excellent three-day seminar on writing screenplays – *Story Structure* – points out that the library is a *gold mine* of information. Where else can you spend countless hours browsing for ideas so productively?

It's interesting to go into a library trying to become informed on a new subject. That's one of the advantages of being a writer

– you never know what you're going to be asked to write about next, and suddenly you have to become knowledgeable on a strange matter very fast. You can even get ideas for books that don't exist. You go in cold, looking for information about a subject. First you look for it yourself, going to the most logical place. If you don't find what you're looking for, then ask at the desk. This is where it gets interesting. The way *you* have the subject categorised may be quite different from the way *they* have.

Take aviation books. In some libraries they're grouped under 'Sports' (*Learning to Fly*), in others under 'Military' (*The Fabulous Spitfire*), in others under 'Transport' (*Civil Airliners of the '80s*). Some even have them under 'Aviation'. The interesting thing about these variations is that you can find yourself unexpectedly looking at books on scuba diving, the Battle of Trafalgar and historical steam engines of the Great Western Railway. Pick one of those up and look through it. Hmm.

When you're doing this browsing, keep looking for connections to your current project or problem. How would *this* affect *that*? Suppose we had a story that did *this*?

In addition to the public libraries, many trade associations and specialist organisations have libraries. These are not always open to the public, but polite asking can usually get you the access you need. The librarians can be very helpful. They can do computer and microfiche searches for you to identify books on particular subjects.

use the Internet for research
the World Wide Web

Anyone who is anyone – organisationally speaking – has a Web home page. You can find almost any information out in a few seconds with a search engine. I use Google (www.google.com), which is excellent at finding keywords in the text of a Web site.

Another good one is Ixquick (www.ixquick.com), which searches 14 conventional search engines and directories (including Yahoo! and AltaVista) simultaneously and sorts through the results to eliminate duplicates.

Once you get to an interesting Web site, you can usually search within the site using its own search engine.

understanding editing

The are several purposes for editing a work:

■ for factual accuracy;
■ for grammatical accuracy;
■ for consistency;
■ for avoidance of repetition;
■ for writing style;
■ for type specification/layout;
■ for space/length requirements.

factual accuracy

Any statements of fact need to be verified. So the first thing to do when reading a text for accuracy is highlight any factual statements, such as: 'Copyright in the United Kingdom is governed by the 1988 Copyright Designs and Patents Act'. When they've all been flagged, they need to be checked by looking at reference works, talking to experts or checking the literature. When did the Wright Brothers make the first flight, was it 17 December 1903 or 1901? An encyclopedia will give the answer (1903).

grammatical accuracy

Let us hope that the writer has more than a rudimentary

knowledge of English grammar. The editor's purpose here is to get rid of any howlers:

■ spelling mistakes;
■ improper punctuation;
■ wrong use of words (eg, affect or effect, principle or principal, there or their);
■ complicated use of too many juxtaposed polysyllabic words;
■ awkward constructions;
■ inconsistencies.

consistency

This refers to spelling and style, particularly if the work is an assembly from several sources. A cohesive work should read cohesively.

avoidance of repetition

This is to avoid lines like 'advertising genius David Ogilvy' being run twice in separate quotes a couple of chapters apart. Or simple repeats of sentences in different sections. Or simple repeats of sentences in different sections.

writing style

Bear in mind what the piece is going to end up as. Is it an article for the house magazine, a business proposal, a brochure? All of these take on a certain style (see Chapter 4). Is the writing you are looking at appropriate? Does it have the right tone of voice? The right gravitas? The right stuff? See page 61.

You may have a house style in which certain rules are established. How does your organisation refer to itself? By name?

'We?' 'The consultancy?' Does the piece conform? Does it reflect your organisation's culture?

Is it good writing? Does it work or does it bore you beyond somnolence? Can it be saved?

type specification

In these days of computers and desktop publishing, speccing type does not occupy much of an editor's time. The basic typography concepts and page layout should already have been decided upon, most likely by an art director or designer. Type specification includes decisions on:

- ■ actual typeface to be used, eg:
  - Times Roman;
  - Helvetica;
  - Courier;
- ■ sizes of the fonts, eg:
  - 10 point;
  - 12 point;
  - 14 point;

–24 point;

- ■ type styles, eg:
  - **Bold**;
  - *Italic*;
  - Underlined;
- ■ setting format, eg:
  - flush left, ragged right;
  -                            flush right, ragged left;
  -                 centred;
  - justified (flush to both left and right margins, like the body copy of this book);
  - use of indents;
  - bullet point format;

- measure (how many picas across the page [there are about six picas to the inch]);
- leading (pronounced ledding) (the spacing between lines of type);
- page structure (where the headers and footers, pagination, etc, go).

space/length requirements

Writing to a required length is an acquired skill. So often it is necessary to make the text fit a specific space. The editor may be found returning the copy to the writer with the request 'cut 12 lines' or 'add two lines' to make it work. It is typically not the editor's job to make these changes. It's back to the writer! The sorts of considerations that must be dealt with are:

- widows (single words ending a paragraph, alone on a line);
- orphans (single words ending a paragraph, alone on a line at the top of a new page);
- sub-heads running at the bottom of the page, with the relevant text starting at the top of the next page;
- picture captions;
- picture placement problems (the need for a picture or chart to be near the relevant text).

accuracy

Accuracy is essential in writing. Once the piece of work is out there it is very difficult to make changes. That's why proof-reading and verification of facts from independent sources is so important. We've all heard the line 'I know it's true; I read it in the newspaper'. And we know how believable that is. Nevertheless, it is your responsibility, as writer, to ensure that what you say is accurate, or if it is supposition or assumption, it is clearly identified as that.

understand © copyright

The dictionary defines copyright as 'the exclusive right to the publication, production, or sale of the rights to a literary, dramatic, musical or artistic work granted by law for a definite period of years to an author, composer, artist, distributor, etc'.

Copyright (©) in the United Kingdom is governed by the 1988 Copyright Designs and Patents Act. Under this, copyright protection of a work extends to 50 years from either the end of the year of publication, or of the author's death, whichever is later. The EU has now extended this period to 70 years.

Copyright applies to all written work, whether it is published or not. The owner of the copyright is assumed to be the author. However, in the case of a person who writes material while on the payroll of an organisation, unless other arrangements have been made, the owner of the copyright is assumed to be the organisation. An example might be a journalist working for a newspaper. Unless otherwise arranged, the newspaper would own the copyright on items the journalist writes that it publishes.

You don't have to 'register' a copyright. It automatically applies. But it is helpful to put a statement of copyright on a work, eg © (owner's name) 2002, such as you'll find on the 'publisher's page' of this book, facing the table of contents.

permissions

If you want to quote from a copyright work you need the permission of the publisher. You may have to pay a fee, which is based on the word count and use to which you want to put it. *The Writer's Handbook* suggests world rights for prose text would run at somewhat under £100 per 1,000 words, with UK and Commonwealth-only or US-only rights being about half that.

Small quotations can usually be granted at no charge, so long as there is acknowledgement of the source.

Now there is nothing standing in your way. Write on!!

index